POSITIVE THINKING
POCKETBOOK

T0087853

POSITIVE THINKING POCKETBOOK

LITTLE EXERCISES FOR A HAPPY AND SUCCESSFUL LIFE

Gill Hasson

CAPSTONE
A Wiley Brand

This edition first published 2019.

© 2019 Gill Hasson

Registered office

John Wiley & Sons Ltd, The Atrium, Southern Gate, Chichester, West Sussex, PO19 8SQ, United Kingdom

For details of our global editorial offices, for customer services and for information about how to apply for permission to reuse the copyright material in this book please see our website at www.wiley.com.

Gill Hasson has asserted her right under the Copyright, Designs and Patents Act, 1988, to be identified as the author of this Work.

Wiley publishes in a variety of print and electronic formats and by print-on-demand. Some material included with standard print versions of this book may not be included in e-books or in print-on-demand. If this book refers to media such as a CD or DVD that is not included in the version you purchased, you may download this material at http://booksupport.wiley.com. For more information about Wiley products, visit www.wiley.com.

Designations used by companies to distinguish their products are often claimed as trademarks. All brand names and product names used in this book are trade names, service marks, trademarks or registered trademarks of their respective owners. The publisher is not associated with any product or vendor mentioned in this book.

Limit of Liability/Disclaimer of Warranty: While the publisher and author have used their best efforts in preparing this book, they make no representations or warranties with the respect to the accuracy or completeness of the contents of this book and specifically disclaim any implied warranties of merchantability or fitness for a particular purpose. It is sold on the understanding that the publisher is not engaged in rendering professional services and neither the publisher nor the author shall be liable for damages arising herefrom. If professional advice or other expert assistance is required, the services of a competent professional should be sought.

Library of Congress Cataloging-in-Publication Data

Names: Hasson, Gill, author.
Title: Positive thinking pocketbook : little exercises for a happy and
  successful life / Gill Hasson.
Description: Hoboken : Capstone, 2019. |
Identifiers: LCCN 2018046260 (print) | LCCN 2018052956 (ebook) | ISBN
  9780857087515 (Adobe PDF) | ISBN 9780857087409 (ePub) | ISBN 9780857087546
  (paperback) | ISBN 9780857087515 (ePDF)
Subjects: LCSH: Self-actualization (Psychology) | Positive psychology. |
  BISAC: SELF-HELP / General.
Classification: LCC BF637.S4 (ebook) | LCC BF637.S4 H368 2019 (print) | DDC
  155.2—dc23
LC record available at https://lccn.loc.gov/2018046260

Cover Design and Illustration: Wiley

Set in 10/12.5pt and Rotis Sans Serif Std Light by SPi Global, Chennai, India

Printed in Great Britain by TJ International Ltd, Padstow, Cornwall, UK

10 9 8 7 6 5 4 3 2 1

CONTENTS

POSITIVE THINKING
POCKETBOOK

INTRODUCTION

Thinking: the talking of the soul with itself. Plato

Is it true that if you can change your thinking, you can change your life?

Yes. It's true.

Anything and everything can be explained in both positive and negative ways. Negative thoughts interpret ideas or events in a pessimistic way and can cause you to get stuck in feelings such as fear, anxiety, disappointment, guilt and resentment. Positive thoughts, meanwhile, can positively influence how you feel and how you respond to situations. In a range of situations and circumstances in your life, positive thinking encourages you to feel capable and optimistic.

A couple of years ago I wrote a book titled *Positive Thinking: Find happiness and achieve your goals through the power of positive thought.* A number of people got in touch to tell me how much they'd gained from the book; that one way or another, they could see how learning to think positively would be a game changer for them – that positive thinking could effect a significant shift in their current way of doing and thinking about things and change their lives for the better.

Readers said that they particularly liked the practical activities and exercises, tips, techniques and strategies. This book, *Positive Thinking Pocketbook* includes many of those activities and exercises, tips, techniques and strategies.

It's the fourth in my series of Pocketbooks. Just like the others, with *Positive Thinking Pocketbook* you can, as one reader wrote '*dip in and out of it and read a page – any page – at a time, so there's none of that discipline needed to sit down and read a whole book properly. Good for lazy people like me!*'

There are four parts to this book.

Part One: Positive thinking vs negative thinking
Part Two: Positive thinking and positive action
Part Three: Making positive thinking a habit
Part Four: Positive thinking for difficult situations

Part One explains the difference between positive and negative thinking and explains why we think in negative ways. It suggests ways to recognise and challenge negative thinking and to move on to more positive ways of thinking.

Can you achieve and get what you want in life simply by thinking positive thoughts? No, you can't. Positive thinking alone won't get you what you want; you can't just think about what you want and how you want things to be and hope to attract it. Instead, positive thinking means being proactive; in a range of situations and circumstances, positive thinking needs to be followed by positive action. The chapters in Part Two explain what you can do to turn positive thoughts into positive outcomes.

Positive thinking requires practice. The more you think and behave in positive ways, the sooner it will become your normal way of thinking and behaving. As well as suggesting positive ways to relate to other people, Part Three explains how small, simple changes to the words you use can make a big difference to the way you think – they can really help you think and behave in helpful, positive ways.

So, does all this mean that if you become a positive thinker, life will always be good? No. Having a positive, optimistic outlook doesn't mean that you are always feeling good and happy. People who are positive still have worries, they still feel sad, disappointed, guilty, angry and so on. But their positive outlook prevents them from getting stuck in unhelpful thoughts and enables them to manage difficulties in a way that doesn't drag them down even further.

Part Four recognises that life is often difficult and sometimes very tough. And that's when you really need positive thinking. In Part Four you'll find a range of difficult scenarios and positive helpful suggestions for managing difficult emotions, disappointments and setbacks, trauma and tragedy.

Positive Thinking Pocketbook has over 100 simple tips, techniques, ideas and suggestions for a wide range of situations where positive thinking can really make a difference. Keep this book in your bag or your pocket for whenever you need to feel more positive. You'll find that the tips, techniques, ideas and suggestions in this book really can help you think and act positively.

As the musician and singer Willie Nelson said, 'Once you replace negative thoughts with positive ones, you'll start having positive results.'

PART 1
POSITIVE THINKING VS NEGATIVE THINKING

UNDERSTANDING THE POWER OF POSITIVE AND NEGATIVE THINKING

Once you replace negative thoughts with positive ones, you'll start having positive results.
—Willie Nelson

Positive thinking can be understood in terms of an 'explanatory style'. Your explanatory style is how you explain situations and events; how you interpret, make sense and meaning of how and why things do and don't happen.

When you interpret an event, a situation or circumstances in a positive way, you take a favourable view of past, present and future events, situations and circumstances. You're likely to look for the best in other people, and to view yourself and your abilities in a positive light. You're optimistic – you expect a favourable outcome for future events. You're not unrealistic though – you know that things don't always work out. But if things go wrong – when there are problems – you don't dwell on them; instead you look for positive solutions. You also look for the silver linings; you recognise that often, challenges and difficult situations have a positive aspect to them.

However, if you have a negative way of explaining and interpreting things, you resign yourself to having no control over or solutions to problems. Negative thinkers are pessimistic – they tend to see and anticipate difficulties and problems. In a variety of situations, if you think in negative ways, you may see yourself as a victim; you feel that you've been deceived or cheated and you look to lay blame when things go wrong. Even when good things happen, negative thinkers tend to notice and dwell on the negative parts – the not so good aspects – of a situation.

Let negative thoughts take a hold, and in a variety of situations, you're likely to feel overwhelmed and powerless. But if you can think positively, you'll feel able to manage and do well.

In Practice

It takes but one positive thought when given a chance to survive and thrive to overpower an entire army of negative thoughts. —Dr Robert H. Schuller

What you think and say to yourself can influence what you can and can't do, as shown by this simple exercise. Try it for yourself. You'll need another person to help.

Part 1:

- Ask the other person to stand and extend their dominant arm horizontally, at shoulder level.
- Ask them to think of a time when they failed something – a test, an exam or a job interview, for example. Then ask them to think negative thoughts about themselves: 'I'm weak. I'm stupid. I'm hopeless. I'm pathetic. I'm no good at anything. I can't do this.'
- Ask the person to continue thinking these thoughts. Tell them you are going to stand behind them and attempt to pull their dominant arm down to their side. Ask them to resist you pulling their arm down.

Part 2:

- Now, ask the person to hold up their dominant arm again at shoulder level.
- This time, ask them to think of a time when they succeeded and did well at something – passed a test or exam, achieved something at work, did well in a sport. Then ask them to think positive things about themselves: 'I do my best. I can do well. I am a good person. I am strong. I can do this.'
- Ask them to repeat the positive statements to themselves while you attempt to pull their arm down to your side. Ask them to resist the pull.

Typically, in the first part of the exercise, the person's arm is more likely to give way to your pull. Negativity overwhelms them and it's not easy for them to be strong. However, when the person's thoughts are positive, their body has the ability to resist the force that's pulling their arm down. They are more likely to stay strong and resist your pull.

UNDERSTANDING THE POSITIVE INTENTIONS OF NEGATIVE THINKING

You are what you think. And what you think, you are. —Author unknown

If positive thinking is the most helpful, beneficial way to think, why, then, do we think in negative ways? Negative thoughts are integral parts of emotions such as fear, anxiety, disappointment, guilt, regret, resentment and jealousy. These emotions often include thoughts such as 'I can't do it'. 'It's not fair'. 'I'm such an idiot'. 'It's *their* fault'. 'Nothing ever goes right for me'. 'I wish I hadn't done that'.

Because emotions such as fear, worry and guilt make us feel bad, we usually think of them as 'negative emotions'. And yet these emotions, like all other emotions, do actually have a positive intent.

Take, for example, the emotion of guilt. Typically, the thoughts that accompany guilt are 'I've screwed up, I shouldn't have done that, it's my fault. I feel bad about what I did'. How can this way of thinking be positive? Well, the positive intent of guilt is to prompt you to recognise your wrongdoing and to do something to put it right or make up for what you did. If, though, you simply wallow in your guilt, berate yourself for what you did wrong or ignore or deny how you feel, then your thoughts and actions (or lack of action) remain negative. They do you no good.

The positive intentions of 'negative' emotions act in the same way as the positive intention of physical pain. If you touch something really hot, the pain makes you pull away; it feels bad, but the positive intention of that pain is to protect you. It's the same with emotional pain – it can prompt you to think of positive ways you can take positive action.

And not only can an emotion such as guilt make you feel bad and prompt you to respond positively, the fact that you *know* that guilt can make you feel bad can actually motivate you, too. It can motivate you *not* to do something in future that could result in you feeling guilty!

In Practice

For there is nothing either good or bad, but thinking makes it so. —Shakespeare

Know that every emotion has a positive purpose. No emotion is bad or pointless. When you experience a 'negative' emotion, if you understand the positive purpose behind that 'negative' emotion, it can help you think more positively about the situation and do something positive about it.

The positive intention of sadness, for example, is to slow you down and allow you time to take in and accept what has happened. Sadness then helps you to adjust, to get used to changed, different circumstances. Disappointment is a form of sadness. The positive purpose of disappointment is to prompt you to identify what went wrong and to work out what needs to be adjusted or changed in order to lessen the chance of similar disappointments in the future.

Think about it.

- Anger is a natural reaction to feeling wronged by something or someone. It's a reaction to unfairness, dishonesty, being treated badly, being let down, being lied to or being ignored. So, what do you think might be the positive purpose of anger?
- Jealousy happens when you feel that someone or something is threatening something you value – you worry that someone will take what you have. What do you think the positive intention of jealousy could be?
- Embarrassment is the feeling of something improper or ridiculous having happened either to yourself or to someone else. What do you think is the positive intention of embarrassment?
- Boredom happens when you lack interest in what's happening – the situation you're in is dull and tedious. What positive aspect might there be, do you think, to boredom? (Answers at the back of the book.)

Try to learn the positive intentions of a range of 'negative' emotions. Then, in any one situation where you experience a 'negative' emotion, you'll be less likely to get stuck in the emotion and be more inclined to think and respond in a positive way.

UNDERSTANDING NARROW AND BROAD THINKING

*Most folks are about as happy as they make up their minds
to be. —Abraham Lincoln*

There is, then, a positive purpose to the 'negative' thoughts that come with emotions such as guilt, fear, anger, sadness and regret. The positive purpose is to focus your attention on whatever 'negative' situation you might be in so that it becomes the *only* thing you can think about and you feel prompted to do something – something positive – to manage the situation. If, for example, you were anxious about missing your flight, you'd constantly check the departures board; your mind would narrow in and focus on the departures board; you'd be unlikely to think of anything else. In another example, if you were worried about a forthcoming exam, your mind would narrow in on what you needed to study and revise in order to pass the exam. Revising for the exam would be a priority and it would be on your mind constantly.

The focused, narrow thinking that comes with 'negative' emotions is negative only if it's unhelpful; if it keeps you stuck, feeling bad and unable or unwilling to do anything to make the situation better.

In contrast, 'positive' emotions such as hope and trust, and the positive thoughts that come with these emotions, can expand your world and the possibilities in it. Positive thinking opens you up to new ideas and new experiences. You feel positive about situations and other people. Hopeful, optimistic thoughts open your mind and allow you to see potential and options in a range of situations.

In Practice

I'd rather have a mind opened by wonder than closed by belief.
—Gerry Spence

Read the scenario below. See how one person's positive thinking opens up possibilities and broadens his ideas, whereas another person's negative thinking limits and narrows his choices, possibilities and opportunities.

Al and Jay had been working for several years as illustrators for a publishing company when they were both offered redundancy. It wasn't a brilliant redundancy package, but Al knew he'd accept. This would be his chance to go freelance.

Al thought about the opportunities and new horizons opening up for him – he thought about how he'd be his own boss, have flexible hours and more control over his days, and be free to pursue the type of illustrative work he was really interested in and liked doing. He thought about how not having to commute to work would give him more time to spend with his wife and children. Al drew up a list of agencies and potential clients and asked for advice and information from friends who already worked freelance. He knew freelancing wasn't going to be easy, but he identified the potential problems and came up with possible solutions, which included a Plan B in case things didn't work out. Al was excited about the possibilities opening up to him.

Jay would also have liked to go freelance, but all he could see were the risks and challenges. 'I don't know how to go about setting up my own business. Supposing I don't get enough clients, what if I'm not good enough?' Jay couldn't move on to identifying solutions to the potential challenges of working freelance. Even though he really didn't enjoy his job – it was stressful, he didn't like his boss and he often worked long hours – he turned down the redundancy.

Jay's narrow, negative thinking limited his options and narrowed his world; his opportunities and choices. It's a negative dynamic – each negative thought narrowed his possibilities and further served to narrow his thinking. In contrast, Al's positive thinking created a positive dynamic: it opened up his mind and broadened his ideas, thoughts and actions. And each new positive thought prompted further positive thoughts and ideas. It's the same for us all – if you think positively, you'll open up your mind and notice opportunities and see possibilities. If, though, you think negatively, your narrow thinking will allow you to see only obstacles and difficulties.

RECOGNISING THE WAY YOU'RE THINKING

Awareness is the greatest agent for change. —Eckhart Tolle

In any one day we all have many, many thoughts which automatically enter our mind and provide us with a running commentary rather like a radio that's permanently tuned to a talk radio station.

These thoughts – your self-talk – direct your actions and behaviour. Some of your thoughts may be positive and constructive – thinking about how to help someone, working out a solution to a problem, looking forward to an event, remembering something good that happened. Some thoughts will be neutral – observations and acknowledgements of day-to-day events: 'It's raining, I'll need an umbrella'. 'I'm hungry. It's dinner time'. Other thoughts – negative thoughts and self-talk – interpret situations and events in a negative way: 'This is never going to work out'. 'Why does this happen to me?' 'They'll think I'm stupid'. 'It's not fair'.

You rarely have conscious awareness of or control over your thoughts, you simply accept them – what your mind says and tells you – and you respond accordingly. That's all well and good if those thoughts are helpful and constructive, encouraging and empowering. But self-talk has a way of creating its own reality, so it's not so good if your thoughts are negative – critical, for example, or fearful or anxious. These sorts of thoughts and self-talk can be limiting, unhelpful, discouraging and self-defeating.

So, one of the first steps in managing negative thoughts is simply to become more aware of them – to identify, in a variety of situations, the way you think and to recognise your 'explanatory style'.

Then, once you're more aware of your negative thoughts, you're in a better position to disempower them.

In Practice

The better awareness, the better your choices. As you make better choices, you will see better results. —Author unknown

Recognise neutral thoughts. Go for a five-minute walk in your neighbourhood or in the area where you work. Once you set off, begin a running commentary in your head describing your walk and everything you notice.

If you don't want to go for a walk, you could simply describe everything in the room you're in.

See whether you can just describe what you see, hear, smell, etc. You're not making judgements. Nothing is good or bad. Your thoughts are neutral.

Get into the habit of noticing your thoughts. Over the next few days, in the morning, write down what your thoughts are about the day ahead. Then set an alarm on your phone to remind you to write down your thoughts at five different times during the day. Or have a note on a computer screen or screen saver that simply asks, 'Thinking…?' Notice whether you were thinking neutral thoughts or positive thoughts or were they judgemental, anxious, apprehensive or blaming thoughts?

When you encounter a challenging situation, notice your thoughts about what's happening. Whenever you're feeling worried, disappointed, stressed, annoyed or upset, stop and become aware of your thoughts. It could be a travel delay, an event that got cancelled, something you lost or something that someone did or said that irritated you. What were your thoughts? How long did you dwell on them?

Ask someone to notice for you. Get someone you like and trust – a friend, partner, family member – to point out, over the next week or so, when they think you've made a negative comment. Write each one down.

RECOGNISING COGNITIVE DISTORTIONS

(Thinking is) what a great many people think they are doing when they are merely rearranging their prejudices. —William James

Negative ways of thinking are often referred to as 'cognitive distortions'. Cognitive distortions are powerful because they can easily convince you that your thoughts *are* rational and true. But actually, they give a false or distorted meaning to situations. They're unhelpful – they can make you feel bad about the world, other people, yourself and your abilities. Cognitive distortions are also known as 'negative thinking traps'. And like all traps, they catch you unaware: you don't even realise you're caught up in thinking this way. Here are some examples:

Confirmation bias. This involves looking for – or simply going along with – evidence to support and confirm what you've already decided is true, while avoiding or ignoring ideas or information that might explain things differently. So, with negative thinking, you give too much weight to negative aspects of a situation and too little attention to the positive aspects.

Tunnel thinking. With tunnel thinking, instead of seeing the whole picture, you focus on the negative aspects only.

Jumping to a conclusion. This involves coming to a conclusion – a negative conclusion – about something before you have all the relevant information.

Polarised thinking. This is 'all or nothing' thinking. There's no middle ground. Things are either good or bad, right or wrong, a success or a total failure.

Catastrophising. When you catastrophise, you think the absolute worst is going to happen in a situation.

Mind reading. With mind reading, you believe you know what the other person is thinking and that their thoughts and intentions are negative.

Blaming. You place all responsibility for something that's gone wrong on someone or something else. You see yourself as helpless, a victim of other people or external factors. But if you self-blame, you place all responsibility on yourself and see yourself as a victim of your own stupidity or lack of ability.

In Practice

Your perspective on life comes from the cage you were held captive in. —Shannon L. Alder

Learn to recognise cognitive distortions and negative thinking traps. Which of these thoughts do you think might be an example of blaming? Which one is mind reading? Which one is catastrophising? Which one of these thoughts is an example of polarised thinking? Which one is confirmation bias and which one is an example of jumping to a conclusion? (Answers at the back of the book.)

- No wonder I've made some mistakes with writing this report. What does my manager expect if she won't give me enough time to complete it properly?
- I bet they only asked me to join them because the other person couldn't make it. They obviously didn't want to ask me first.
- I've never used the tube trains in London before. I'll get confused and stressed. I just know I'll get completely lost. I won't know what to do.
- The person who interviewed me was very nice but all I can think about was the one question I didn't know how to answer.
- My manager has changed her mind and doesn't need the report after all. So that's another example of how incompetent she is.
- My friend hasn't replied to my texts. I must have done something to upset him.
- If this isn't perfect it will have been a complete waste of time.

REWIRING YOUR BRAIN

Not only does behavior change the structure of the brain through neuroplasticity; just thinking about or imagining particular behaviors can change brain structure as well.
—John B. Arden

If you're in the habit of thinking negatively, it helps to understand what's going on in your brain.

The core components of the brain are neurons. Neurons are cells that process and transmit information and they're connected to each other by neural pathways and networks.

When you think or do something new, a new neural pathway is created. Then, each time you think or do something in that particular way, your brain uses that same neural pathway. The pathway becomes stronger and stronger each time it's used. It's just like walking through a field of long grass – the more often that path is trodden, the more established the path becomes and the more likely it is that you'll take that path.

This is of great benefit to you because it means that if you do something often enough, it becomes automatic – a habit: you don't have to think about it. Think, for example, of the things you do on a daily basis that your brain and body are so used to, they don't have to think about them – walking, talking, eating, brushing your teeth, driving, texting, etc.

However, this same process of neural pathways developing automatic ways of thinking and doing also establishes habits that are not so good for you: smoking, overeating, drinking, negative thinking and so on. If you often interpret events in a negative way, then you create strong negative neural pathways in your brain. Those neural pathways become so established that they also become habits: negative thinking habits.

The good news is that if you change how you think or what you do – if you think and behave in more positive ways – then new neural pathways are formed. When you continue using these new pathways, they become stronger. Eventually, they will replace the old ways of thinking and behaving. You will have rewired – or reprogrammed – your brain.

In Practice

If you change the way you look at things, you change the way you look at change. —Wayne Dyer

Rewire your brain. Try doing things differently and see how it's possible to retrain your brain.

Get a piece of paper and if you're right-handed, use your left hand (your non-dominant hand) instead of your right hand; if you're left-handed, use your right hand. Do the following:

- Draw a square.
- Draw a circle.
- Draw a triangle.
- Write the numbers 1 to 10.
- Write your name.
- Write the following sentence: 'I'm writing this sentence with my non-dominant hand'.

Now use your non-dominant hand to do one of the following every day for a week:

- Brush your teeth.
- Make your tea or coffee.
- Open doors.

It will take time and effort because the neural pathway for using your right hand is well established. But if you really want to do it, you can forge new neural pathways and develop the ability to do things with a different hand. You can retrain your brain.

It's the same process for establishing positive ways of thinking – it takes time, effort and commitment to think in more positive ways, but it is possible and it's never too late. In fact, the more of the tips, strategies and ideas for positive thinking you use from this book, and the more often you use them, the quicker and more easily you will be a positive thinker!

CHALLENGING YOUR THOUGHTS: ARE THEY HELPFUL?

Be careful how you talk to yourself because you are listening. —Lisa M. Hayes

Imagine you're given a parrot. This parrot is just a parrot – it doesn't have any special knowledge, wisdom or insight. It recites things 'parrot fashion' without any understanding of what it's saying. It's just a parrot.

However, this particular parrot has been trained to be unhelpful to you – continuously commenting on you and your life, putting you down, doubting your decisions, criticising, berating and blaming you and other people.

For example, one day you get stuck in a traffic jam or the train or bus is delayed and you're late. The parrot sits there saying, 'You should've left home earlier! What's the matter with you? You can't do anything right. It's not a good start to the day... squawk, squawk, squawk.'

Another time, a friend has said they'll text you this week to arrange to meet up at the weekend. It's Saturday morning and you haven't heard from them. The parrot tells you, 'You can't rely on your friends. They can't be bothered with you.'

Of course, you know there's no point arguing with the parrot – he's just reciting his lines.

But when it comes to your negative self-talk, you *can* challenge what you say to yourself – you can question how reasonable, logical and helpful your thoughts really are.

In Practice

Tell the negative committee that meets inside your head to sit down and shut up. —Ann Bradford

In any one situation, ask yourself, 'Are these thoughts helping me?' Ask yourself, 'Is what I'm thinking helping the situation?' Think whether your thoughts make you feel good or bad and do or don't get you what you want.

Try to remember a difficult, stressful event or situation you experienced recently. Maybe you lost something? Did someone criticise you or let you down? Perhaps you had a long travel delay? Maybe an event got cancelled, or you had a frustrating phone call with someone at a call centre – an insurance company, TV and broadband, gas or electricity provider. Whatever your thoughts were, did they in any way help and make the situation easier?

Now think of an upcoming event you're not looking forward to – some work or a household chore you have to do, somewhere you've got to go, someone you have to meet and talk to. Whatever it is, what are your thoughts about it? Are they helpful? Are your thoughts helping you to feel better about the situation?

Think of something you would like to do in future – travel somewhere, take up a new interest or hobby, change your career direction, leave a job or relationship – but haven't done yet. Is the way you're thinking about it helpful? Are your thoughts giving you hope and motivating you to get going?

Know that when you ask yourself 'Is this thought helpful?', you're not disputing the accuracy of your thoughts; you're not arguing with yourself as to whether or not the person at the end of the phone was or wasn't being rude or that the reason you haven't left your job is because you think no one else will want to employ you.

Regardless of their accuracy, these thoughts probably aren't helping you; they're not making you feel good and they're not making your life easy.

CHALLENGING YOUR THOUGHTS:
ARE YOU CERTAIN?

If you don't like your world, question your thoughts about it. —Byron Katie

How often have you been quite certain about something, only to discover that what you believed wasn't true, that you were in fact mistaken or even completely wrong?

Maybe, as a child, you thought as I did, that all dogs were male and all cats were female. I once read about a teenager who believed her brother when he told her that all bank notes are made from dolphin skin; that's why, he said, bank notes feel different to normal paper. Someone else thought that laughter tracks on TV comedy shows were actually the sounds of other people laughing in their homes all over the country, being broadcast 'live'. She used to sit near the TV and laugh loudly so she could hear herself on TV. And someone else I read about described how, when she was little, she was terrified of getting on high-speed trains. She stood on the platform while they screamed through the station and assumed that it was like that inside the train, too.

Maybe you once discovered that the lyrics you'd been singing for years were, in fact, completely wrong. Someone I once knew was surprised to discover that the lyrics to Blondie's chart-topping hit 'Denis' were not, as she'd been singing, 'beneath the knees' but 'Denis Denis'. And someone else told me they thought that a line in Queen's 'Bohemian Rhapsody' was 'Saving his life from this warm sausage tea'. The correct lyric? 'Spare him his life from this monstrosity'.

Ridiculous? Yes. Yet when it comes to your own thoughts about yourself, other people and the world, you probably believe they are all rational and valid. It rarely occurs to you that your thoughts about events might be illogical, unreasonable or just plain wrong!

How, then, can we be certain that anything we think or believe is true? There is, after all, always more than one way of thinking about yourself, other people, events and situations.

In Practice

There are no facts, only interpretations. —Friedrich Nietzsche

Remember the story of 'The emperor's new clothes'? A dishonest tailor promises to make the emperor the most fabulous outfit for the next public occasion. The emperor gives the tailor a bag of gold to buy the beautiful, rare fabric that will be required and the tailor gets busy. When the emperor comes for his fitting, the tailor tells him that only the cleverest, wisest people can see the exquisite materials that this outfit is made of, so very pure and delicate are they. The emperor, naturally, is not about to admit that he is not among the cleverest, wisest people, and so he says not a word as the tailor helps him into the new clothes.

The great day arrives and the royal procession makes its way through the streets. The crowds cheer and commend to each other the beauty and elegance of the emperor's new clothes. All, that is, except one small boy, who calls out so all can hear: 'Why is that man not wearing any clothes?'

Often, it takes only one question to challenge the certainty of what you believe. Remember that!

Which of these 'facts' do you believe are true? On a scale of 1–10, how certain are you?:

- Bananas grow on trees.
- You can't see the Great Wall of China from space.
- Bats are blind.
- All your fingernails grow at the same rate.
- Your kneecap is the roundest part of your body.
- Things will never be as good as they used to be.

Question the certainty with which you feel your thoughts are absolutely right. Challenge your thoughts by asking yourself questions that can help you recognise that there's more than one way to think about things. Ask yourself questions such as 'How do I know this?' 'What's the evidence to support what I think?' 'On a scale of 1–10, how certain am I?' 'What evidence might there be for a more helpful, positive way to think about this?'

IDENTIFYING ALTERNATIVE PERSPECTIVES

Our life is what our thoughts make it. —Marcus Aurelius

Recognising that the way you"re thinking isn't helpful or reasonable can help you to loosen your grip on what you think you're certain of. And when you're not so certain about something, you're more likely to be open to other possibilities. Positive possibilities!

There's always more than one way to look at things. You can prove this to yourself. Just ask other people what they think about some of the subjects on the list below and see how, for any one subject, there's more than one belief or point of view.

The Royal Family	McDonald's
Chewing gum	Sushi
Brussels sprouts	Dark chocolate
Online dating	Cats
Blue cheese	New Year's Eve parties

In Practice

Only you have the power to change your thoughts. Alter your thoughts and you alter your world.
—Miranda Kerr

See someone in a different light. Think of someone you've always found difficult to get on with – a family member, the friend of a friend, a neighbour, a colleague or the prime minister. Put aside your beliefs and opinions about them and see something new about them. Look for something positive. It could be an aspect of their personality, their attitude or what they wear. It could be something about the way they interact with others or something about how they work.

See something in a different light. Which of these chores don't you like doing? Washing dishes, ironing or cooking? Perhaps you don't like doing the laundry, vacuuming or taking out the rubbish? Perhaps you hate changing bed linen? What is it about those chores that you don't like? What would be an alternative way of thinking about them? Vacuuming and cleaning windows can be thought of as a way of doing physical exercise. Washing up and ironing can be seen as an opportunity to listen to music or a podcast.

Recognise that there *are* alternative ways of thinking. If you find this hard, try taking a step back and depersonalising the process. Think of yourself as a script writer and imagine you are simply writing alternative thoughts and lines for a character in a play. Just be sure to keep them plausible and realistic enough for you to believe them.

Throw your thoughts away. In any one situation, once you have an alternative thought that you *can* believe, write the negative thought on a piece of paper, then tear it up or screw it up and throw it in the bin. Or text it or write it on your computer, then press 'delete'.

MOVING ON TO POSITIVE THOUGHTS

Negative thoughts stick around because we believe them, not because we want them or choose them. —Andrew J. Bernstein

Cognitive behavioural therapy (CBT) techniques – identifying, challenging and replacing negative thoughts – have been found to be very effective in helping people to think more positively. Another approach, 'Acceptance and Commitment', suggests that although you need to be aware of negative thoughts and to recognise when they are unhelpful, you don't necessarily need to challenge them. Instead you simply notice them, accept them and let them go so that you can move on to more helpful ways of thinking, responding and behaving.

So if, for example, you thought, 'The waiter is deliberately ignoring me', you don't challenge that thought – you don't ask yourself how sure you are and what the evidence is that he's ignoring you. Instead, whether your thinking is correct or not, you simply acknowledge and accept that it's not helping you to continue thinking in this way and you move on to thinking – to committing yourself to – more helpful thoughts and solutions. So, in this example, you'd think about how you could more effectively get the waiter's attention.

Acceptance and Commitment recognises that when you accept and let go of negative, unhelpful thoughts, you let go of the emotional aspects and allow the rational, logical part of your mind to start working for you – to think in more helpful, positive ways.

In Practice

God grant me the serenity to accept the things I cannot change; courage to change the things I can; and wisdom to know the difference.
—Reinhold Niebuhr

Instead of getting caught up with your thoughts and struggling with them, just notice them and let them go. Imagine you're a sheriff in an old Western town. You notice an outlaw strolling down the main street. You don't challenge him, you simply acknowledge the outlaw and then calmly and firmly encourage him to keep walking, right on out of town. You can do the same with negative, unhelpful thoughts – notice them and allow them to keep moving along out of your mind. Instead of challenging your negative thoughts, you simply acknowledge and release them. If and when they come back, look them in the eye like that sheriff and tell them what they need to do – keep moving along.

When you notice negative thoughts are entering your mind, say 'stop!' to yourself. If you're alone, you can say it out loud, but it's also effective when you just say it in your head. Images can help – for instance, a bright red stop sign that you picture in your mind's eye when intrusive thoughts begin to appear.

Use a thought-changing prompt. When you notice that negative thoughts or images are starting to enter your mind, to prompt you to come up with alternative, more positive, helpful thoughts, try one of these:

If you're sitting down, stand up.
If you're standing up, sit down.
If you're indoors, go to a different room.
If you're outside, change the direction you're walking – take 20 steps in the opposite direction before turning round and going back the way you were going.

PART 2
POSITIVE THINKING AND POSITIVE ACTION

HAVING GOALS

You are never too old to set another goal or to dream a new dream. —C.S. Lewis

Is positive thinking unrealistic? Some people think it is. They think that you can't achieve your goals and get what you want in life simply by being positive and optimistic. They're right.

Positive thinking alone won't get you what you want in any one situation. Positive thinking will not 'attract' positive events from the universe – you can't just think about what you want and hope to attract it. Instead, positive thinking involves being proactive: you've got to *do* something!

In a range of situations, positive thinking needs to be followed by positive action.

Positive thinking encourages proactive behaviour and enables you to come up with pragmatic and creative ways to accomplish goals. So, if you combine positive thinking with positive action, you'll be more likely to get positive results.

Having goals and aims and working towards achieving them helps to develop positive thinking because it gives you a positive path to follow. And the positive path generates positive thoughts, which in turn encourages further positive action.

It's a positive dynamic: a win-win situation!

In Practice

Setting goals is the first step in turning the invisible into the visible.
—Tony Robbins

Think of something you'd like to do, something you'd like to achieve. It could be a short-term goal – something you want to achieve in the next few days or weeks – or a longer-term goal – something you want to achieve in the next few months or years. Maybe it's to do with your health – you might want to lose weight, stop smoking, take up running or simply be able to walk up a hill without being out of breath.

It could be something you'd like to learn or improve – play a musical instrument or learn a language.

Maybe it's something to do with work – get promoted, or reduce your hours, work freelance, return to study or do some voluntary work.

Perhaps you want to travel, visit New York or New Zealand? Perhaps you just want to be able to get out of your own front door – you've been struggling with a mental or physical health issue and you'd like to get to the local shops and back without too much stress.

It could be that you have a problem to sort out – you want a less cluttered home, or you want to manage a difficult person, leave your job, a university course or a relationship.

Or maybe you want to act, be a standup comedian, write a book, join a band or a choir, make new friends, grow your own vegetables or decorate a room in your home.

Identify the benefits. Whatever it is, why is a particular goal important to you? In what way will you benefit from achieving your goal? Although to some extent you may feel your goal will be challenging, first and foremost your goal should inspire you. It's not difficult to be inspired, you simply need to identify the benefits – what you stand to gain from working towards and achieving each goal. And if your goal is an issue or problem that you want to deal with, think about what the result or outcome will be – what do you see yourself doing once the problem has been solved?

IDENTIFYING YOUR OPTIONS

The most common way people give up their power is by thinking they don't have any.
—Alice Walker

Whatever it is you want to do – whether it's something specific, like losing ten kilos or finding a part-time job, growing your own vegetables or learning to dance a tango, or something more general, such as travel or be more healthy or learn a new language – more often than not there's more than one way to achieve it.

You have choices.

Identifying a range of options will stretch you beyond your usual way of thinking, and because positive thinking broadens and opens up possibilities and ideas, you may find that some of your ideas spark other ideas.

Too often, though, you might spend ages agonising over the pros and cons of each option: you over-think the situation. How, you might wonder, do you know that you'll be choosing the best option, that you'll definitely be making the 'right' choice and the 'best' decision? How to know that the option you choose will work out, and if it doesn't, that you won't regret having made a different decision?

Quite simply, you don't, can't and won't. When you make a decision, you can never know for sure that it's going to turn out well. But with some thought and positive action, you can make it more likely.

In Practice

Take time to deliberate, but when the time for action comes, stop thinking and go in. —Napoléon Bonaparte

For each option, ask yourself some questions and write down your answers.

- What are the pros and cons for each option?
- What skills, strengths and resources do I currently have that could be helpful for each option? What further information do I need?
- Who could help: who could give me advice, ideas or practical help? What resources might I need?

Accept uncertainty; make a choice despite possible unknowns. Know there is no 'right' or 'wrong' option. When you're finding it difficult to make a decision, for each option ask yourself: 'What's the worst that can happen? How might I deal with that?' Know that you can make a choice and if things don't work out, you will already have thought of what to do to manage what happens.

Make a well-informed decision, but know that the pursuit of more information can be a way of putting off a decision. Trust your intuition. When you feel strongly that a particular path or choice is the right one, know that it's because your decision is in line with your aims and values. Don't wait until conditions are perfect, get started now. If new information comes to light after you have decided which option to follow, if necessary you can alter your course then.

TAKING POSITIVE STEPS

How do you eat an elephant? One bite at a time. —Author unknown

If you have something you want to achieve, you might be feeling daunted or discouraged by how little time you have and how much effort you've got to put in. You may, for example, be up against a deadline – you have only a few days to write a presentation for a meeting next week.

Maybe, though, you're not concerned with how little time you've got to achieve something. It could be that you're more concerned with how long something is going to take before you achieve it – how long it's going to take you to learn a language, for example, or decorate a room or even renovate the whole house.

But whether you're short of time or it's going to take a long time, the most helpful and effective approach is to break things down into small, doable steps. Taking a step-by-step approach is the most positive way forward because it means you set yourself up for constant successes by achieving small targets along the way.

Just start with the first step. Focus only on that step and complete it. Then move on to the next step. And then the next one. Each step may or may not be challenging in some way. But if it does feel overwhelming or too difficult, break down that step into a few smaller steps.

Even with the steps that you find challenging, you can recognise that every task you complete brings you closer to the ultimate goal. If, for example, you're decorating a room and you dislike sanding down woodwork, you simply keep in mind that once you've completed the sanding, you're one step closer to the room being finished.

Doing things one step at a time also gives you time to look at what is working and what isn't, and to decide whether you need to change tactics. So, as you go through each step, review the outcome. What worked? What helped and went well?

In Practice

The man who moves a mountain begins by carrying small stones.
—Chinese proverb

Remind yourself that any goal, task or project becomes doable as a series of smaller steps. It's something you've done many times before. Any task, activity or goal, anything you've achieved – making a cup of tea, having a party, passing your driving test or moving home – has been as a result of a series of steps.

Write down all the things you think you'd need to do towards your goal. Just empty your mind. You don't need to write things down in any particular order just yet. If, for example, you wanted to change your career, the things you'd need to do might include talking to a careers advisor or coach, spending time online researching jobs and training in the career you're interested in, and rewriting your CV. These are all part of the larger goal, but breaking them down makes them easier to think about and to work on.

Next, make a written list, outlining your steps. What's the first step you can take? What will be the next? Once you get started on your aim or goal, it'll be easier to get straight on to the next step because you'll already have planned what and how you are going to do it. Remember that you're aiming to think positively. Tell yourself, 'I have a plan. I can manage this'. Just know to focus on one thing at a time. And each time you achieve a small part of your goal, you'll feel a sense of achievement and see yourself getting closer to getting what you want.

Be flexible. Of course, some goals have an inherent deadline – if you want to learn to dance a Cha Cha for your wedding in two months' time, you can't really change that date. What you can do, though, is give yourself a flexible plan to follow – increasing the amount of practice if you need to – rather than have the pressure of a deadline looming.

USING POSITIVE VISUALISATION

The future you see is the future you get. —Author unknown

Often, when you're planning to achieve something, you visualise it first. If, for example, you're planning a trip to a city in another country, you might imagine yourself going from your home by car, train or bus to the airport. Then you'd visualise the time you'd spend at the airport and then the flight. You'd then imagine yourself arriving at your destination and heading over to the car hire place. You'd then see yourself arriving in the city and making your way to your hotel.

When you visualise in this way, it's like someone is going ahead of you and beating a path for you to follow – they've prepared the way ready for when you come along in that direction; the path has been made easier for you.

This process of visualising and imagining is useful to help you plan anything you want to do, to 'see' the steps. It also alerts your brain to be aware of and to recognise any resources, information, ideas and opportunities that could help you to achieve your goal as you work towards it.

Furthermore, if you can imagine yourself achieving something, your brain then believes and accepts it *is* indeed possible and that you *can* do it. But if you constantly visualise *not* being able to do something, your brain believes and accepts that, too. Your brain can't tell the difference between having visualised making that journey 50 miles away, for example, or having done it for real. If your brain thinks you've done something successfully once, it's more likely to think – to believe – you can do it again. And that's positive thinking!

In Practice

As a striker, you're always visualising where and how you could be scoring goals against the opposition. —Marcus Rashford

Use positive visualisation. There are two parts to visualisation: outcome visualisation and process visualisation.

Outcome visualisation involves seeing yourself reaching your goal – you create a detailed mental image of what it is you aim to achieve. If, for example, your aim is to run your first marathon, you'd visualise yourself crossing the finish line, exhausted but exhilarated. You'd see your family and friends greeting you and congratulating you. You'd imagine all the excitement and the enormous sense of achievement.

The second, crucial part of positive visualisation is process visualisation. It involves imagining each of the steps you'll take towards your goal. So, if it was a marathon, you'd visualise yourself starting off, running well, arms relaxed, breathing controlled. In your mind, you'd break the course into sections and visualise running each part, thinking about your pace, breathing and split time. You'd imagine what you'd do if you hit 'the wall', the point where your body and mind are simultaneously tested to the point of wanting to give up.

You may never run a marathon. However, you can use the same principles to achieve any goal. Create a strong image of yourself succeeding. Then picture what you must do during each step towards your goal and, like a runner pushing through the wall, imagine how you will manage and overcome obstacles or setbacks.

Write it down. Writing down your goal, or drawing a picture of the steps and achieving them, is another way of visualising. As you describe or draw the steps and what you will achieve, you are automatically visualising.

BEING FLEXIBLE

Be clear about your goal but be flexible about the process of achieving it. —Brian Tracy

Whatever goal or goals you have, whatever you want to do and however you've chosen to go about it, your plans don't need to be fixed.

As you work towards something you want to achieve, you'll need to be flexible and open to the fact that problems are bound to arise. So being prepared to change course in light of the unexpected means that you avoid limiting your chance of success by focusing on just one way to accomplish it.

Suppose you are planning a meal that you are going to make for your friends. You decide on what you'll cook for the main course and for a dessert. You write a shopping list and you go to the supermarket. You find all the ingredients except one. It's a vital ingredient. What to do? Do you cancel the meal? Of course you don't. You decide what your options are and what you're going to do next.

It's the same approach with setbacks to anything you set out to do – you identify what, exactly, the problem is and then you look for a solution. You might be able to deal with the problem or you might conclude that Plan A isn't, after all, going to work out. So you abandon that and switch to Plan B.

Whether it's a meal, travel plans, changing your job, getting fit or improving a relationship with a friend or family member, things can get in the way. The weather changes, a road is closed, someone you were relying on drops out, you fall or sustain an injury, or it costs more money than you expected. But if you really want to get what you want, there's always a way. And most likely, there's more than one way.

In Practice

If Plan A doesn't work, the alphabet has 25 more letters. —Author unknown

Plan for difficulties. When you're at the planning stage, anticipate potential problems and possible solutions. For each step, think about what could go wrong. What's the worst that could happen? What might the potential problems be? Think how you could deal with that. Who could help? What support, advice, finances or resources could you draw on?

Asking yourself questions like these is not to discourage you and put you off doing what you want to do. On the contrary, it's making it more likely you'll be successful. How come? Because you've anticipated the potential problems and you've already thought through how you would deal with them. Forewarned is forearmed!

Have a plan B. If, when you were planning how to achieve your goal, you looked at all your options, you'll already have identified a Plan B, an option that you can implement if the original one proves impractical or unsuccessful. Furthermore, having a Plan B can also encourage you to go out on a limb and take a risk. Why? Because you'll know what you'll do if Plan A doesn't work out.

Know that it's okay to change course. Don't be afraid to admit a decision was a bad idea or isn't working out. If you stick to Plan A at all costs, you could miss opportunities.

GETTING MOTIVATED

People often say that motivation doesn't last. Well, neither does bathing, that's why we recommend it daily. —Zig Ziglar

Whether you're aiming to improve your health, take more exercise or eat more healthily, learn a new skill – a language, or something practical – move home or leave a relationship, whatever it is you're aiming to achieve it's quite possible that despite your good intentions, you just can't get yourself started.

You might think, 'It'll take too long to achieve' or 'It's going to be too hard' or 'It's going to be scary'. It could be that you think, 'I don't have the skills or ability,' 'I might not do it right' or 'My friends might not like it or my family will disapprove'. It's true, it might be too hard, it might be scary, other people might not like it and they could disapprove.

There will always be challenges and difficulties. But, if you stay where you are – stuck in negative, unhelpful thoughts – and, if you don't push yourself, nothing will change.

You can sit and wait for everything to be just right, but nothing is ever going to happen until you actually start getting on with it. As Sir Isaac Newton discovered, objects at rest tend to stay at rest. But objects in motion tend to stay in motion. This is just as true for feelings as it is for falling apples!

So how to get the motivation to start? By thinking positively, of course! And by doing something positive to get you started.

In Practice

Life is like a ten-speed bicycle. Most of us have gears we never use.
—Charles Schulz

Keep in mind the good reasons. Motivation involves having a reason for wanting to do something. What's your reason to achieve something? Why is it so important to you? How will you benefit, what will you gain from achieving what it is you want? Maybe it's a financial or material gain. Perhaps it's personal gain – you'll be happier or wiser, or you will learn something new, be more healthy or improve yourself or your situation in some other way. Whatever it is, keep it in mind. Even better, write it down and pin it up where you can see it every day, or set up your phone to send yourself a regular reminder.

Commit to just a short period – just five minutes, ten minutes, half an hour – of positive action. Whatever it is – filling in an application form, writing an essay or report, going for a run, decorating or decluttering a room – decide that you'll just spend a short time on it. Decide that you'll simply fill in part of the application form, write the introduction to the essay, run round the block, paint one wall, declutter one drawer, etc.

Don't wait till you feel like doing it. Instead, start doing something immediately, without thinking and giving your mind time to come up with excuses and you talk yourself out of it. After a short time, the positive feelings which you need to keep going will start to emerge naturally. You may well find that once you get going, you end up continuing well past the short period you'd decided on.

Set things up for yourself. Whatever it is you want to do, spend a minute or two setting it up so that it's easier to get going. Want to go for a swim or a run each morning but can't get your act together? Put your swimming costume or running gear on before you get properly dressed. That way you're far more likely to make a start.

STAYING MOTIVATED

It is always during a passing state of mind that we make lasting resolutions. —Marcel Proust

Do you make new year's resolutions? More to the point, do you keep them?

Maybe you don't make resolutions because you know it's unlikely you'll stick with them. You're not alone in thinking like this – studies show that around 80% of people break their resolutions within six weeks of making them.

While making unrealistic resolutions, or allowing self-doubt or old habits to start creeping back in, can sabotage our efforts, a key reason many of us fail to keep to our resolutions and achieve our aims is that we lack the strategies and techniques needed to stay the course.

So, whether you make resolutions on January 1st or any other day of the year, you need to work out a strategy that will help you deal with flagging motivation and will keep you on track.

In Practice

Life is like riding a bicycle. To keep your balance, you must keep moving. —Albert Einstein

Remind yourself of the good reasons. Whenever you feel yourself flagging, remind yourself of the benefits – what you stand to gain by achieving whatever it is you're aiming for.

Make it fun. Find ways to make anything you're aiming for interesting and fun to do. Maybe it's something you could do with someone else. Things that are difficult to find the enthusiasm to do are especially tedious when doing them alone. Whatever it is – getting fit, losing weight, learning a new skill – partner up and get it done together.

Do it somewhere different. If, for example, it's something you can do on your laptop, go to a café, library, garden or park and do your work from there.

Reward yourself for your progress. Before you get started, think of something you'll reward yourself with. Each time you complete a step, give yourself a treat. Yes, this is how you train a dog, but it will work for you, too.

Try a reverse reward. Give your friend a sum of money – £10, £50 or £100. If you achieve your goal, you get your money back. If you don't complete it, you lose it. They then get to donate it to a charity of their choice.

Try the 'if…, then…' technique. This involves attaching something you want to do regularly to something you already regularly do. In other words, you link a new habit to an already established habit. For example, you might cook a meal every evening. You might also be learning a language. So you could link the cooking with the learning. '*If* I'm cooking, *then* I'll listen to a language lesson'.

If you wanted to get fitter, you might decide, '*If* I need to go up a couple of floors at work, *then* I won't take the lift, I'll walk up the stairs. *If* I'm taking the bus or tube, *then* I'll get off one stop earlier. And *if* I'm using the car, *then* I'll park 10 minutes from my destination and walk the rest of the way'.

USING POSITIVE BODY LANGUAGE

I speak two languages. Body and English. —Mae West

Recent research suggests that the way you sit and stand – your posture and other aspects of your body language – can actually affect the way your brain functions. For example, awkward, uncomfortable, uptight gestures and body language will leave you feeling and thinking the same way.

Carry yourself with confidence and in a matter of minutes, the chemical balance – the testosterone and cortisol levels in the brain – alter. Your body starts to feel it and your brain starts to believe it.

The good news is that you don't have to learn a whole new repertoire of poses, gestures and expressions that feel unnatural or uncomfortable. Adopting just a couple of positive poses or gestures or ways of speaking can make a big difference to how you think and feel.

If you can focus on maintaining just those two or three things, you'll find that the rest of your body and mind will match up and you will feel more confident and thus come across as more positive and confident.

In Practice

Our bodies change our minds, and our minds can change our behaviour, and our behaviour can change our outcomes. —Amy Cuddy

Read through this list of actions and choose two that you would find most comfortable to adopt when you want to feel more positive and confident:

- Stand or sit straight.
- Keep your head level.
- Relax your shoulders.
- Spread your weight evenly on both legs.
- If sitting, keep your elbows on the arms of your chair (rather than tightly against your sides).
- Make appropriate eye contact.
- Lower the pitch of your voice.
- Speak more slowly.

You can't control *all* your non-verbal communication; in fact, the harder you try, the more unnatural you're likely to feel. But if you can keep your mind on doing one or two of those things consistently, your thoughts, feelings and behaviour can match up.

Which one or two actions would you feel comfortable using? Practise using them right now!

PART 3
MAKING POSITIVE THINKING A HABIT

BEING APPRECIATIVE

Before we value anything, the fact that we value anything at all, is because we have first seen it and registered its value. —Alex Ratcliffe

Think of the times you've bought something new – a phone, a computer or a bike – and been really pleased with it. Maybe it was some new shoes or a coat? Or some new furniture, a new home or a car.

How long was it before the initial thrill wore off?

How about the times you got a new job, or you were given a pay rise? How soon before the job and the higher earnings became your new normal?

Think of the last time that something you thought wasn't going to go well didn't turn out badly after all – maybe the medical tests you were so worried about came back negative, a work deadline was extended unexpectedly or a social event you didn't want to go to was cancelled. How long did the feeling of relief last?

When positive events like these happen in our lives, they give us a real lift, but within a short while we adapt to the situation and we don't think of those things in the same positive way as we did when we first owned or experienced them. We simply take them for granted; we no longer appreciate them.

The 20th-century psychologist Abraham Maslow suggested that 'getting used to our blessings is one of the most important non-evil generators of human evil, tragedy, and suffering'. This may be an extreme view, but the principle is true: failing to pay attention to and appreciate the good things in your life can leave you believing that you're lacking and missing out and that your lot in life is not so good.

It doesn't have to be this way!

Appreciate the things you already own. Make a point of noticing and acknowledging the benefits and pleasures your things have brought you, so that your pleasure in them doesn't wear off. Remind yourself of what's gone right and turned out well.

In Practice

I think if we took more time to stop and think how lucky we are and focus on these things we often forget to appreciate, we'd be happier. You and I should try that. —Ilona Burton

Think of the things you do, have or own that pleased you when you first had them. Stop to reflect on those things now. Think about how useful/helpful/nice they still are. Remind yourself how pleased you were when you first got them.

Appreciate three things. At the end of each day, think of three things that went well. You can simply reflect on what those things were at the end of the day – while you're brushing your teeth or as you go to sleep – or you may want to write down what those three good things were in a notebook.

They only need to be small, simple things – perhaps, for example, you ran for the bus or train and managed to catch it a few seconds before it pulled off. Or you managed to fix something, a cupboard door or a knot in a necklace. Or you found something you thought you'd lost. Maybe you cooked something new and everyone liked it. Or you ate a perfectly ripe peach. Or you had a good hair day. It could be that your dog did something that made you laugh, or you received a humorous text from a friend, or perhaps something made you laugh so hard that you made no sound at all.

Whether you've had a good day or not, identify and reflect on the small things that happened. Doing this not only helps train your mind to think positively, but if you've had a bad day, you're learning how to identify the positive despite difficulties and disappointments. So no, you didn't get offered the job or a place on the course, but at least they did give you some helpful feedback. And although your team lost, there were no hold-ups leaving the stadium and getting back home.

Appreciate that you had good in your day so that whatever else happened, you know you did have things that made it all worthwhile. Do this before you go to bed every night and no matter what happened that day, you go to bed in a positive frame of mind.

BEING KIND

You cannot do a kindness too soon because you never know how soon it will be too late.
—Ralph Waldo Emerson

What does it mean to be kind? It means doing or saying something to make someone else's situation easier – less difficult – or simply adding something positive to someone else's day.

Being kind to other people creates a positive mindset – it gets you into a cycle of positive thinking and behaviour. Why? Because when you make an effort to be kind, you have to actively look for opportunities to be kind: to think and to act in positive ways.

People appreciate kindness – when you show care, concern and support to others, you're likely to get a positive response. This means you both feel good – the other person feels good because of your kindness and you feel good as a result of the other person's response. And even if they don't acknowledge your kindness, *you* know you did good!

We all have innate kindness and compassion, but sometimes it takes a reminder to tune into it.

You need to be only a bit aware of other people to start seeing opportunities to help. It doesn't have to cost anything or take much time. It can be little things that don't take too much effort; the smallest gestures can make a big difference – an offer of a cup of tea, an invite to dinner, or an offer to help someone with a task or chore. You'll lift their spirits and see yourself making a positive difference at the same time.

Think about what you might do to show some kindness and you'll be more likely to spot opportunities when they come up – when, for example, you notice someone in need, someone who could do with a kind word or gesture.

In Practice

A single act of kindness throws out roots in all directions, and the roots spring up and make new trees. —Amelia Earhart

Remind yourself to be kind. Write a note that says: 'Be Kind'. Place it on the wall above your desk or on the fridge to remind you. Make the words 'Be Kind' a screensaver on your phone.

Never underestimate the power of small gestures. Start someone else's day with a smile. Send a text to a friend or family member saying 'Morning! How's things with you?' Hold the door open for someone and smile at them as you do. In a supermarket queue, let the person who seems rushed go in front of you. And on the road, be kind to other drivers; in a queue, let people merge in.

Do a chore that you don't normally do, for someone else. Make the tea, cook, shop for food, fill or empty the dishwasher. Take the rubbish out, clean the loo, get the car cleaned, change the ink cartridge in the printer.

Be inclusive. Encourage others to join you in something and be part of something, to be involved in what you're doing or talking about. Invite people out. Ask someone to do something nice with you – the cinema, a show, a walk, a meal. If you hear about an event – an exhibition, a film, a band, a show, a street party – or a new café, pub or restaurant that you think someone you know would enjoy, ask them if they'd like to go to it with you.

Contact someone you know who is going through a difficult time. Phone or write them a card, email or text, cook a meal or send flowers or some other thoughtful expression to let them know you care and are thinking about them.

'Pay it forward'. If you receive a kindness today, let it be the prompt to do something kind for someone else.

BEING GENEROUS

Generosity isn't about money, it's about the heart. —Author unknown

We can probably all agree that generosity, like kindness and appreciation, is a good thing. A positive thing. But what does being generous really mean? Like kindness, being generous involves gestures that make someone else's life easier, less difficult. But being generous means being liberal in giving or sharing; it means giving *more* than might be expected.

You have an opportunity to be generous whenever you're aware that extra effort on your part could make all the difference. Being generous often involves putting others before yourself. It's generous of you, for example, to take the sofa and let your friend sleep in the bed when they stay over at your place. You didn't have to do that! But by going one step beyond what's expected of you, you're being generous.

You have an opportunity to act generously whenever you see someone in need and you are able to help. You can be generous to others with your time, your money, your possessions, your energy and your skills. You can be generous with your support, help and encouragement. You can also be generous – magnanimous – with your forgiveness.

In Practice

For it is in giving that we receive. —Francis of Assisi

Be generous with your time. Whether it's ten minutes or an hour or two, spend some extra time with someone who needs it or will appreciate it. Someone who is lonely, needs help with learning or understanding something.

Don't sell your things, give them away. Have a clear-out and rather than sell your things on eBay or Gumtree, give away some of them via www.freecycle.org.

Give it away. Does a friend love something you own? Give it to them.

Go the extra mile. Literally. Go out of your way to give someone you know who needs it, a lift.

Give more. Whether it's donating money to a friend's justgiving.com page for a fundraising event they're involved in or being your friend's gym partner as they try to get fit, helping someone reach a goal by giving more time or money than they expect is a generous thing to do.

Give a generous tip. It could make someone's day.

Provide the best biscuits. If you have someone working in your home – an electrician, plumber, builder, decorator, someone to repair the washing machine – offer them more than a cup of tea. Buy some really nice biscuits or cake and offer those, too.

Graciously accept from others. Let others do things for you. Being overly independent or self-denying excludes others from the opportunity to contribute and feel good for having done so. Yes, it might be quicker to do it yourself, but without being patronising, be generous – accept their offer of help.

MAKING A CONTRIBUTION

Everybody can be great. Because anybody can serve. You don't have to have a college degree to serve… You only need a heart full of grace. A soul generated by love. —Martin Luther King, Jr

As well as being kind and generous to other people in your life – friends, family and colleagues – another positive way to make a difference to other people's lives is to give some of your time to a national or global cause or to a local community initiative that interests you – an issue, cause or initiative that you identify with or that you feel strongly about.

Whether it's supporting adults to learn to read, mentoring young people, supporting ex-offenders, advocating for people with mental health problems or visiting elderly people in hospital, you'll be able to make a difference. A positive difference. And it's not only people whose situations you can help improve – you can also help animals. You might get involved in a national organisation such as Cats Protection or the Guide Dogs for the Blind Association, or you might want to help out at your local hedgehog sanctuary.

Perhaps you'd like to get involved in an environmental initiative – Greenpeace, for example, which works to promote the protection of world ecology and the natural environment. Or you could volunteer with the National Trust – maybe as a conservation volunteer or volunteer wildlife surveyor, surveying a range of different habitats, helping to monitor biodiversity. There are also opportunities to help less mobile visitors by driving them in a mobility buggy, allowing them access to parts of gardens, woods and grounds that otherwise they would not be able to see.

Whatever you choose to do, volunteering your time and energy, your skills and abilities can positively affect the people you help. But it can have a number of positive effects on you, too. Through volunteering you can try something different, learn new skills and experiences, discover hidden talents and achieve new things. You can feel part of something good and worthwhile. Volunteering can help you meet different kinds of people and make new friends. As someone once said, 'Plant flowers in others' gardens and your life becomes a bouquet!'

In Practice

Volunteer. Go to www.do-it.org where you'll find a list of a wide range of voluntary opportunities in your local area. You can find out about being a court volunteer for your local witness service, or being a 'collector', someone who collects surplus food donated from partnering supermarkets for local foodbanks. You'll find opportunities to be a 'social buddy' for adults with learning difficulties, or to work in your local Oxfam bookshop, or to be a 'health walk' leader through your local council.

Save a life. Donate blood. Donated blood is a lifeline for many people needing long-term treatments, not just in emergencies. Your blood's main components – red cells, plasma and platelets – are vital for many different uses. Go to www.blood.co.uk. You can also help those who need a transplant. Sign up to the organ donor register and donate your organs and tissues. It takes two minutes to fill in the form online. Go to www.organdonation.nhs.uk.

Speak out. There are people in our world who need someone to speak out for them. You don't have to take on that cause by yourself, but join others. It could be Amnesty International – a global movement of more than 7 million people who take injustice personally – or it could be speaking up at a local council meeting, writing letters and otherwise making a need heard.

Divert one specific expense for a set of time – a week, a month – to a charity or cause. You could choose to bring a lunch to work, or to give up a coffee. Donate the money you save to a specific charity or cause that you feel strongly about – the environment, child welfare or animal rights, the Red Cross, or a cancer or Parkinson's charity.

GIVING COMPLIMENTS

A pat on the back is only a few vertebrae removed from a kick in the pants, but is miles ahead in results. —Bennett Cerf

Compliments, like appreciation, kindness and generosity, crystallise positive thinking. Why? Because giving praise and compliments encourages you to see the best in people, to be aware of and to comment on their good efforts, choices and intentions.

When you give praise, express admiration, congratulate someone, show appreciation or simply say 'thank you', not only does it let the other person know that their efforts or actions have been noticed, it shows that you have made an effort, too – you have made the effort to acknowledge their actions.

A compliment can encourage the other person to keep doing whatever it is you're complimenting them on. And a compliment is an even more powerful encourager if the other person has been struggling or just is unsure about their efforts and actions.

Don't worry about getting the wording just right and so end up not saying anything. A genuine sentiment phrased a bit awkwardly is better than saying nothing at all.

Not only can a compliment brighten someone's day, it can do the same for you. Next time you're feeling low or cranky, take a look around and see who you can compliment. If you can just let someone know you like something about them – whether it's their smart shoes, their neat handwriting or their ability to be patient in a particular situation – tell them. You could end up transforming their day and your own!

In Practice

Acknowledge personal qualities or special efforts. Be specific. Sometimes the most memorable compliments are the most specific ones because they show that you were paying attention. You might, for example, comment on the way a person successfully handled someone else: 'I admire your patience, it's great that you stayed so calm with that difficult customer. Good on you!'

Explain what a difference their efforts have made. People feel good if they know that they made a difference. So, if what they have done has had a positive effect on you, tell them! For example, 'I feel like I really learnt something from seeing how you managed that. Thanks'.

When you tell the other person that they've made a positive difference, they can then feel good about themselves and encouraged because of the impact their actions had on you.

Notice what someone is wearing and how they look. Compliment people on their homes. Be specific – don't just say 'what a nice home' or 'you look nice'. Add what, specifically, is nice – their hairstyle, or the furniture they've chosen.

Notice the work someone does. It could be someone who goes out of their way when they're serving you in a shop or café. Make a positive comment about their service, their work or their business. Let a manager know when you get great customer service, too.

Put it in writing. When it's appropriate, putting it in writing – an email, text or hand-written note – shows even more effort on your part while also giving the person a permanent reminder of the praise. Getting positive reviews can make a big difference for a small business. So, if you went to a fun event, or you love your local independent restaurant, leave a positive review.

And the next time you read something that encourages or motivates you, let the writer know. Make a comment on a website or blog; let them know how they helped or inspired you with their book, website or blog. Write a positive review or comment.

INDULGING IN SMALL PLEASURES

I'd rather have roses on my table than diamonds on my neck. —Emma Goldman

Small pleasures are a big deal! A small pleasure might be a short-lived pleasure – a passing happiness – but a small pleasure can give you an instant positivity boost.

The big pleasures of life – landing a great job or a promotion, getting a place at university, buying a new home, going on holiday, having a baby you've been longing for – are certainly important. We spend a lot of time and effort working towards those goals and the happiness of having achieved something big can be great. But these big joys don't happen every day. The small joys are different – they can keep coming our way as often we make them or notice them.

What, for you, makes for small pleasures? A bubble bath, a hot shower, warm towels? Fresh clean sheets? Reading a book by one of your favourite authors, watching a great film or playing loud music and singing along to it while you cook dinner? Maybe, on a cold morning, it's putting on an item of clothing that's been sitting on a hot radiator? Maybe eating the froth on the cappuccino is one of your small pleasures.

What about having breakfast in bed or eating last night's leftovers for breakfast? Or slurping hot soup on a cold night? Maybe you like watching daytime TV when you've got a day off sick. A kiss, a cuddle or holding hands? Perhaps it's an open fire, the smell of freshly cut grass, sitting in the sun or a walk in the rain? Maybe talking to your dog or cat is one of your small pleasures.

Life is a collection of moments and the more happy, positive moments we have, the more often we are happy and positive.

In Practice

Look out for what makes you smile and surround yourself with it as much as you can. —Ilona
Burton

Be mindful; make the effort to notice what's happening around you that pleases you. When you make an effort to notice things, you'll be surprised at just how many things make you smile and lift your spirits.

Get into the habit of identifying and indulging in small pleasures – the ordinary and the extraordinary, the familiar and the new, the small things and the bigger things. The cheap and the expensive, the easily accessible and the things that are hard to find or to come by. Canadian author Neil Pasricha has managed to identify 1000 small pleasures. Here are a few that might resonate with you:

- Perfect parallel parking on the first try.
- High-fiving babies.
- Absolute perfect silence.
- Car dancing.
- The first shower you take after not showering for a really long time.

Neil has listed all of his 1000 small pleasures on his website. Go to 1000AwesomeThings .com to read them and find some more that might inspire you too.

Collect positive, inspiring quotes, poetry and song lyrics for different situations in your life. Read them when you need a shot of positivity.

Remember someone or something that made you laugh. Listen to or watch five minutes of something that makes you laugh – a YouTube clip from a comedy programme, or a standup comedian.

Identify a few things you own that you love. They could be mementos, ornaments, pictures, photos or letters that spark joy and make you feel good.

Make time in your working day for small pleasures. Have something to look forward to each lunchtime – something healthy to eat and a small treat. You could get some exercise, go for a run, a walk, a swim or cycle. Go for a manicure or a blow dry. Phone a friend or a family member for a chat.

Plan for things to look forward to. Whether it's a day or a night out with friends, a weekend away, a holiday or an adventure, get something booked and put into your diary or calendar, even if it's weeks or months from now. Then, whenever you need a shot of happiness, remind yourself about it.

USING MORE POSITIVE LANGUAGE

Words create worlds. —Pierre du Plessis

The words we use and the things we say have the power to make us feel good about ourselves, other people and our world. But the words we use and the things we say can also limit and confine us and make us feel bad ourselves, our situations, our world and the other people in it.

As the 19th-century American novelist Nathaniel Hawthorne said, 'Words: So innocent and powerless as they are, as standing in a dictionary, how potent for good and evil they become in the hands of one who knows how to combine them'.

Be more aware of the words you use. It's okay to pause mid-sentence and organise your thoughts so that you can phrase them – and what you say out loud – in a positive way. Writing letters, emails and texts provides the perfect opportunity to work on positive language, as you can think about and edit your words before sending. But if you do catch yourself using a negative word or phrase out loud, then just as you can when you're writing, stop and rephrase what you want to say in more positive terms.

Small, simple changes to the words you use can make a big difference to the way you think – they can really help you think and behave in helpful, positive ways. Just remember, your self-talk can be positive, kind, encouraging and empowering, so be more conscious – and conscientious – about the words you use; frame your thoughts in positive words and language.

In Practice

The mouth speaks what the heart is full of. —Author unknown

Replace 'won't' with 'will' and 'can't' with 'can'. Telling yourself what you do want rather than what you don't want puts the focus on what you want to happen rather than on what you don't. It increases your chances of a positive outcome.

Instead of saying what you *can't* do, say what you *can* do. For example, rather than saying 'I can't do this till tomorrow', a more positive way of expressing this would be to simply say, 'I can do this tomorrow'. In another example, instead of saying, 'I won't get there for another hour', it would be more positive to simply say, 'I will get there in an hour'. And instead of 'I won't be able to let you know until the end of the week', leave out the word 'won't' and instead simply say 'I will let you know at the end of the week'.

What do you think is a positive alternative to this sentence? *I can't come and see you until next week.*

Beware of 'never', 'every' and 'always'. Words like 'always' and 'never' are often misused because the statements that include them are rarely true. For instance, 'I always forget things' is probably not true. You don't always forget things really, do you? It would be far more realistic to say, 'I often forget things' or 'I sometimes forget things'.

Words such as always, never, all, every – everybody and every time – are known as 'universal quantifiers'. They are generalisations that tend to create feelings of frustration, disappointment, resentment and unworthiness. They're often used in an accusatory, argumentative or self-pitying way. For example, 'You never listen to me'.

Always and never statements are always false and never true.
—Author unknown

Add the word 'yet'. If things aren't quite happening the way you want them to, simply adding 'yet' to the end of a sentence can create a more positive mindset. Consider the impact of 'We've not got any orders' compared with 'We've not got any orders yet'.

The 'yet' tells you that something hasn't happened up till now but there's still time; there are still possibilities and opportunities. It encourages you to be hopeful and to look for a solution.

SAYING 'BUT' OR 'AND'

Words are containers for power, you choose what kind of power they carry. —Joyce Meyer

Simple tweaks to the words you use can make a big difference to your mind-set – to how you think, what you say and what you do. Look at these four sentences, each of which starts with some positive words:

- 'I went to the shop and got everything we needed *but* I forgot to buy the milk'.
- 'Thanks for washing up, *but* you didn't put everything away or wipe down the counter'.
- 'I went for a run *but* I only managed to get round the park twice'.
- 'It's nice of them to invite me to dinner *but* it was probably because some-one else dropped out'.

'But' is a minimising word that devalues the positive words before it. In these examples, by using the word 'but' you've taken away from the fact that you *did* buy the other things you needed, the other person *did* do the washing up for you, you *did* run round the park twice and it *was* nice of them to invite you for dinner.

Replacing the word 'but' with 'and' creates a much more positive meaning. By using 'and', you make it more likely that you will also come up with a positive solution. 'But' is final. 'And' implies there's still more to come, as you can read here:

- 'I went to the shops *and* I forgot to buy the milk so after lunch I'll go back and buy some'.
- 'Thanks for washing up *and* if you could just put those things away and wipe down the counter, that would be perfect!'
- 'I went for a run *and* I managed to get round the park twice. Tomorrow I'm going to try to do three times'.
- 'It's nice of them to invite me to dinner *and* I'm looking forward to it'.

Each time, the word *and* compels you to complete the sentence in a positive way.

How could you make this sentence more positive by using 'and' instead of 'but'?

'There may be lots of fish in the ocean *but* I'll never catch one that's right for me'.

'There may be lots of fish in the ocean and…'

In Practice

Words have the power to make things happen. —*Frederick Buechner*

It works the other way round, too. Take this sentence: 'I'm so unfit *but* I can exercise and get fitter'. This time, the sentence started out as a negative thought, but got turned into a positive thought with the word 'but'. This time 'but' encourages you to complete your sentence with something positive. In fact, if you could just add a 'but' to every negative thought you produced, you could transform so many negative thoughts into positive ones!

'I'm nervous about going to the party, *but* I do know a couple of people who are going, so I will have someone to talk to'.
'They didn't offer me the job *but* they gave me some helpful feedback'.

What, do you think, might be a positive ending for each of these sentences?

'I don't like living here but…'
'I'm fed up with my job but…'
'I've let my friend down by cancelling our night out together, but…'

The more often you can add a 'but' to a negative thought, the more often you turn it into a more helpful, positive one.

What's a negative thought you've had that you can turn into a positive one with the simple use of the word 'but'?

'I _____ but _____.'

SAYING 'SHOULD' OR 'COULD'

Handle them carefully, for words have more power than atom bombs.
—Pearl Strachan Hurd

Do you realise just how insidious the words 'should' and 'shouldn't' can be? They may appear to be harmless enough – simple words in a sentence – but actually they have an unhelpful or even harmful effect. Telling yourself that you 'should' be doing something is telling yourself that you *ought* to – even though it's very likely that you don't *want* to. Furthermore, when you think that you 'should' be saying, doing or feeling something, you are disapproving of yourself. Although you feel guilty, you're *still* not saying, doing or feeling it!

If you're thinking about what others 'should' or 'shouldn't' be doing, you're expressing disapproval about what they are or are not doing and probably feel frustrated and resentful when they don't comply with what you've suggested.

Even if you're trying to motivate and encourage someone else, as well-meaning as you might be, when you tell them that they 'should' or 'shouldn't' do something or feel a certain way – you're putting pressure on them. You're suggesting they're doing something wrong if they do or don't say, do or feel something.

So, as you might imagine, there are very few situations when the words 'should' and 'shouldn't' evoke a positive response!

In Practice

Be sure to taste your words before you spit them out. —Author unknown

Instead of saying 'should' or 'shouldn't', try using 'could' instead. Using the word 'could' instead of 'should' suggests that you – or someone else – do, in fact, have a choice about whether to do something or not. This shift in use of words is a more positive, flexible approach to thinking, saying, feeling and doing things. Rather than suggesting that you ought to or should do something – which adds pressure that creates negativity – you are making a choice about what to think, say, feel and do. So, for example, instead of telling yourself 'I should stop what I'm doing and get to work', try saying 'I could stop what I'm doing and get to work'.

Invite yourself to do something rather than tell yourself you should. Instead of telling yourself that you 'should' do something, ask yourself whether you *want* to do something. For example, instead of 'I should do more exercise', ask yourself, 'Do I want to do more exercise?'

Take responsibility; own what you think and how you feel. Instead of telling yourself, for example, 'I know I *shouldn't* feel like this but I really don't like that person', admit, 'I *do* feel like this, I *don't* like that person'. And instead of telling yourself, 'I shouldn't be thinking like this', face facts: recognise that you *do* think like this.

Whenever you find yourself saying 'I should', ask yourself, 'What would happen if I didn't?' 'I should go and visit my elderly relative'. Or 'I should get out of the office into some fresh air at lunchtime'. When you ask, 'What would happen if I didn't?', you're prompted to consider the consequences of doing or not doing something.

And in response to statements like 'I shouldn't', ask yourself, 'What would happen if I did?' For example, 'I shouldn't keep eating so much junk food'. Ask yourself what would happen if you did continue to each so much junk food.

Listen to the people around you and to people talking on the TV and radio. Be aware of how and when other people use 'should', 'shouldn't', 'can't', 'must' and 'mustn't'. Do their words create a positive or a negative approach? Listen out for other people's negative words and phrases and think of positive alternatives.

BEING MORE CONFIDENT

Success comes in cans, not cant's. —Author unknown

Confidence – self-confidence – is not about what you can or can't do. It's what you *think and believe* you can or can't do.

When you're feeling confident, you believe that you *can* do things; you have a positive attitude towards yourself and your abilities and you believe that events and experiences are likely to turn out well.

Conversely, when you're not feeling confident, you're likely to believe that things will turn out badly. You may even feel that there's no point in trying. When faced with a new challenge or opportunity, if you lack confidence you probably think to yourself, 'I can't do that' or 'I'll fail' or 'I won't be any good at this. I'll be hopeless.' You discourage yourself and give up before you've even started.

Your negative thinking – jumping to conclusions, catastrophising, tunnel thinking, etc. – undermines your confidence and makes you believe that you can't do certain things. If you don't believe in yourself and your abilities, in a range of situations, you risk feeling bad about yourself – you will have low self-esteem. And that just undermines your confidence further and you feel bad again. It's a negative dynamic.

But if, when challenges and setbacks occur, you're feeling confident, you're able to work towards overcoming the difficulties. You're likely to think, 'I'm going to give this a good try' or 'I can start again' or 'I'll do the best I can'. Your positive thoughts help you to believe that you *can* do things and things can work out. It's a positive dynamic!

In Practice

We ask ourselves, Who am I to be brilliant, gorgeous, talented, and fabulous? Actually, who are you not to be? —Marianne Williamson

Start from a position of strength. Instead of focusing on what you believe you can't do, focus on what you *know* you can do and what makes you feel good about yourself. Here are a few ways that you can do this:

Do more of what you enjoy. What do you like doing? Are there activities in your life that bring you a sense of satisfaction and make you feel good about yourself and your abilities? Whatever those activities are, do them more often. It could be, for example, something to do with your job, voluntary work, a hobby or interest, family and friends. Doing more of what you enjoy, and that you're good at, can help build your confidence and increase your self-esteem. Why? Because you not only *believe* these are things you like and do ok at, you *know* it, too. And when you reflect on the activity – when you think back over what you're doing and have been doing – you feel good about yourself and your abilities in that area.

Identify your qualities and strengths. Put the words 'positive qualities' into a search engine. Find five words that describe you. Then write a few sentences for each word, describing how you know you are, for example, patient, reliable, caring, fun and open-minded. Make these your personal, positive affirmations, truths about yourself that you **can** believe and feel good about yourself for. Write them down and keep them where you can read them as and when you need to.

Build your confidence. Do one small thing every day that scares you just a little and feel your confidence and courage grow. Identify something you'd like to feel more confident about and take small steps to achieve it. Whatever it is, although it may present a challenge, it shouldn't be too difficult. For example, you might like more confidence to speak up at work. You could, therefore, decide, 'I'll just ask one question in this afternoon's meeting'. Make it even easier for yourself: ask a nice person!

BEING WITH POSITIVE PEOPLE

I always tell young girls, surround yourself with goodness. I learned early on how to get the haters out of my life. —Michelle Obama

Throughout our lives we come across all kinds of people, different in many ways. But when it comes to the impact and influence they have on us – our mood, motivation, confidence and self-esteem – other people can fall into one of two camps: they're either 'radiators' or 'drains'.

People who are radiators spread warmth and positivity, while drains can leave you feeling, among other things, discouraged, disappointed or angry, guilty or resentful. They drain your energy. Their misery, criticism and complaining can overwhelm you.

It's not always possible or practical to switch off from negative people or to remove them from your life completely. What you can do, however, is be aware of the effect their negativity is having on you and as much as possible reduce the amount of time you spend around them. When you do encounter them, afterwards take some time to re-energise yourself.

Who you spend most of your time with can make a big difference to the way you think, feel and behave.

You need radiators – positive people – in your life! Positive people are likely to respond to you in positive ways and so make you think positively about yourself and the world around you.

In Practice

Surround yourself with people who make you happy. People who make you laugh, who help you when you're in need. People who genuinely care. They are the ones worth keeping in your life. Everyone else is just passing through. —Karl Marx

Who are the positive people in your life? Which people come to mind from the list below?

- Someone who makes me feel good about myself.
- Someone I can totally be myself with.
- Someone who values my opinion.
- Someone who tells me how well I am doing.
- Someone I can talk to if I am worried.
- Someone who makes me laugh and I can have fun with.
- Someone who shares an interest or hobby with me.
- Someone who introduces me to new ideas, interests or new people.
- Someone who is generous with their time, ideas or resources.

You may have a different person or a number of people for each situation, or the same one or two people might fit a number of situations. Think widely; the positive people on your list do not just have to be friends or family, they could be colleagues or neighbours.

The person you can talk to if you're worried, for example, could be a professional person that you see, such as your doctor, a counsellor or someone from an organisation with a helpline. Maybe the person who introduces you to new ideas and interests is a writer. Perhaps there's someone on the radio or TV who makes you laugh. The person who inspires you could be someone you've read about who has overcome adversity or who has achieved something despite all the odds.

CONSUMING POSITIVE NEWS

Out of the 10,000 news stories you may have read in the last 12 months, did even one allow you to make a better decision about a serious matter in your life? —Rolf Dobelli

In an essay on his website www.dobelli.com the writer Rolf Dobelli explains how in recent years, many of us have recognised the effect on our health of consuming an abundance of food. 'Today', he says, 'we have reached the same point in relation to information that we faced 20 years ago in regard to food. We are beginning to recognise how toxic news can be'. He goes on to explain how reading and listening to panicky stories triggers the release of the hormone cortisol and our bodies find themselves in a state of chronic stress. Dobelli says, 'News feeds the mother of all cognitive errors: confirmation bias. In the words of Warren Buffett: "What the human being is best at doing is interpreting all new information so that their prior conclusions remain intact."'

Dobelli say that news stories 'are overwhelmingly about things we cannot influence. They grind us down until we adopt a worldview that is pessimistic, desensitised, sarcastic and fatalistic'.

The author Steven Covey agrees. In his book *The Seven Habits of Highly Effective People*, he explains the concepts of the 'Circle of Concern' and the 'Circle of Influence'. The Circle of Concern is the area over which we have no control – the economy, for example, war and terrorism, the behaviour of celebrities and political scandal – but that you can waste time and energy getting worried about; stressed, helpless and negative simply *because* you have little or no control over these events. The Circle of Influence, meanwhile, is the area over which you *do* have control. It involves the issues and events that you *can* influence in your daily life – your goals, your attitude, the skills you develop, what you learn, what you read, listen to and watch, what you eat, the exercise you take and so on. You can do something about the issues and events in the Circle of Influence. And when you give most of your time and energy to your Circle of Influence, you are likely to feel more positive about yourself because you can initiate and influence change.

In Practice

If you want to fly, you have to give up the things that weigh you down. —Author unknown

Minimise the amount of negative news in your life. Most of us have a number of sources of information that we could eliminate from our day with no detriment to our lives whatsoever. While staying up to date can keep you informed and enable you to take part in discussions, it can also mean your life is filled with irrelevant or unnecessary information. News and information overload are to the mind what sugar is to the body: empty calories that give you a rush but then bring you down and leave you feeling like crap. You wouldn't want to stuff your body with low-quality food. Why fill your mind with low-quality thoughts?

Read more positive news. Instead of consuming whatever is readily available, and drains you, make more conscious choices about what you read, watch and listen to. Watch and read motivational stories or speeches. TED talks (www.ted.com), for example, are inspiring, educational and motivating.

Online, you can find websites dedicated to sharing inspiring and positive news from around the world, such as the following:

www.dailygood.org/
www.huffingtonpost.com/good-news/
www.goodnewsnetwork.org/
www.positive.news
www.sunnyskyz.com/

Steer clear of negative headlines and dire tales of things going wrong. Look instead for uplifting stories that celebrate the best of life and be inspired by the good in the world around us.

PART 4

POSITIVE THINKING FOR DIFFICULT SITUATIONS

MANAGING DISAPPOINTMENTS AND SETBACKS

There's a bit of magic in everything, and some loss to even things out. —Lou Reed

It's easy to be positive when things are going well in your life. The real challenge to positive thinking comes when problems, setbacks and disappointments occur. Unexpected financial difficulties or health problems, other people blocking you or withdrawing their support, for example, can easily set you back.

Being turned down for a place on a course, a job, a flat or a house are all sources of disappointment. So is seeing your team lose, or bad weather upsetting your plans, or failing an exam, or a bad meeting at work or a social occasion not going as well as you'd expected it to.

Even if you're trying to forget about it, a disappointment can stay hovering in the back of your mind like a grey cloud. This is a perfectly natural response to the hurt and sadness that occur when your expectations or hopes fail to materialise. If you're upset or disappointed about something, it's not because you're not positive enough, it's because you're human.

Whenever a situation leaves you feeling disappointed, you need to sit with it; to take time to acknowledge and accept that what has happened *has* happened and nothing can change that. You then need to see what there is to learn from your disappointment and move on.

Of course, it's not always easy to do this. Negative thinking, dwelling on what failed to materialise – the place on the course, for example, or the sale that didn't go through, or the celebratory meal that wasn't as good as you were expecting it to be – can keep you stuck and unable to move past the disappointment. But all the time you allow yourself to brood on what did or didn't happen, you make it difficult to move forward, to think logically and clearly – to think positively.

In Practice

You have to be able to get up and dust yourself off and always be going forward. —Rita Moreno

Release yourself from thinking how things 'should' have been. It's too easy to remain disappointed if you're still attached to how things 'should' have been. It's not helpful. As long as you are trapped in what you think should or shouldn't have happened, you prevent yourself from doing anything constructive about the situation. Once you've acknowledged your expectations, you need to let go and move on. And sometimes, that might be in a different direction.

Think like a sports fan. Sports fans and participants know that whenever they or their team lose, staying stuck in disappointment is not helpful. They let go of negative thinking and instead move on to think about the next game or race and the opportunities it will present. In order to leave disappointment behind, you must do the same – make a decision that you are going to move on.

Focus on thinking about what can be done rather than what wasn't or can't be done. Be open to new ideas and new ways of doing things. Rather than thinking, 'I should/shouldn't have…', try saying, 'It might help to…' or 'I could…' or 'Now I'm going to…'.

Think back to the last time that you were disappointed. What did you learn? Did you even stop to reflect on this? By reflecting on what happened and what went wrong, you can identify what you've learnt that will help you avoid similar disappointments and setbacks in the future.

Anticipate future disappointment. Having a Plan B will not only help you feel less vulnerable, it will also lessen the disappointment if things don't work out. Supposing the weather turns cold and rainy and you can't have the BBQ party you planned for that evening. If you've already thought what you'll do if the weather turns bad, you can still go ahead with the party, just not quite in the way you originally planned.

BEING STUCK IN A JOB YOU DON'T LIKE

Oh, you hate your job? Why didn't you say so? There's a support group for that. It's called everybody, and they meet at the bar. —Drew Carey

In a 2012 study by the polling and management consulting firm Gallup, only 13% of people said they were 'engaged' in their work, that they found it meaningful and looked forward to it.[1] Most people though – 63% – were unhappy; they were 'not engaged' at work, they felt no real connection to their job. A further 24% hated their job.

Are you stuck in a job you don't like? Perhaps your work is meaningless and dull; you're bored and unchallenged. Perhaps you feel it's beneath you? Or is it that your job is stressful; you feel overworked and unappreciated? Maybe you hate your boss and don't like your colleagues, clients or customers.

Perhaps you can't afford to leave – you're not sure that you could get another job that pays the same or is as close to home. Is it that you're receiving on-the-job training and you don't want to leave until you've completed it? Whatever the reason, much as you want to, right now you can't quit.

Could it be, though, that you're looking at the elephant's rear end?

There's a story about three blind men who were asked to describe an elephant. Each stood at a different part of the elephant's body and described what they thought an elephant must look like, since that's all they knew from their particular point of view. Sometimes a job is just like that elephant – you see it only from where you are and how you feel. You miss what else might be there.

---

[1] https://www.gallup.com/services/178517/state-global-workplace.aspx

In Practice

Beware of confirmation bias. The more you dislike your job or aspects of your job, the more you might look for evidence to back up your dislike. Instead, look for the positive aspects. Is your job close to home and so you have a short journey? Is your commute a long one but you get to listen to the radio in the car or you can read, listen to a podcast or watch something on your phone on the train? Your boss might be awful but maybe your colleagues are great?

Make your job work for you. Instead of making yourself miserable railing against the things you can't change, look to see what you can change and control. Perhaps you could negotiate a day working from home? Or maybe you could reduce your hours? If you think you could manage on less money, reducing your hours can mean less time at work and more time to pursue other interests. You'll feel less defined by the job and have more time to look for other positions and attend interviews.

Take control of your professional and personal development. Choose an aspect of your job that's particularly difficult, boring or irritating and set yourself a challenge to make it less difficult, boring or irritating. Maybe, for example, you have a job where you often have to manage complaints – employees' or customers' complaints? Take it on as a challenge – learn how to be really good at managing and resolving complaints.

Perhaps you could take the lead on initiating changes and improvements at work – a more comfortable working environment, or more efficient methods and procedures, or a flexible working policy?

What would you like to do in your next job? Is there a skill you'll need that you can develop in this role? Whatever it is, do what you need to do to get really, really good at it and make it as much a part of your job as you can. If you can't develop new skills and challenges related to your work, then look for other ways you can learn new skills online, on a course or through voluntary work, in your lunchtime, on your commute, in the evenings or at the weekend.

SURVIVING TRAUMA AND TRAGEDY

The paradox of trauma is that it has both the power to destroy and the power to transform and resurrect. —Peter A. Levine

When you've been through the kind of event that devastates your life, that overwhelms you with shock and grief, the last thing you can think about is being positive. Whether it's serious illness, being involved in an accident or a terrorist attack, a bitter divorce or bereavement, how can there possibly be an upside?

Finding something positive doesn't mean denying how tragic and devastating the situation is, but it can help prevent you from being overwhelmed by the awfulness of it.

Just as with a disappointment, with trauma and tragedy you'll need to give yourself time to acknowledge and accept that what has happened *has* happened. The sadness and shock that come with grief are intended to slow you down and allow you to reflect and take in what has happened, to accept that there's no turning back – nothing and no one can change what has happened. At some point, though, when you can, focusing on who and what has been helpful and supportive can begin to steer your mind in a positive direction.

Research has found that trauma can be a powerful force for positive change. In the 1980s, University of North Carolina professors Richard Tedeschi and Lawrence Calhoun discovered that more than half of the trauma survivors they interviewed reported positive change – they believed that their lives had eventually changed for the better. They had experienced what Tedeschi and Calhoun described as 'post-traumatic growth'.

Among other things, the people who had experienced trauma in Tedeschi and Calhoun's study felt that they had become wiser, stronger, more empathic and accepting of others, had developed closer relationships and had more compassion for others. Many had re-evaluated their priorities, had a greater appreciation for things in their life, had identified new possibilities and, often, had become more spiritual.

In Practice

Sometimes in tragedy we find our life's purpose. —Robert Brault

Know that even during the worst of times, there can be something to be thankful for. Most of the time it's not obvious. You have to look, and often you have to look hard. You can help yourself to cope better in difficult times by training yourself to look for the positive in your everyday life.

On page 45 you will have read about identifying and reflecting on three positive things that happened in your day. If you can get into the habit of doing this in your normal daily life, you will have established a habit that will serve you well when you're faced with really tough times and serious adversity. It won't change what's happened, but it may help you not to be overwhelmed by it.

Reflect on the positive. If you've experienced a traumatic event, it may help to think about what you've learnt about yourself.

- What inner strengths did you discover and draw on?
- Has your experience given you an empathy and understanding for other people when they are faced with adversity?
- How might you use what you've experienced and learnt to help yourself and other people or to create something of personal or social value?
- What might you do differently – what new opportunities might there be now? What new relationships?
- How might you interact with people differently?

Know that growth and hope can coexist with grief. Of course, months and even years later, you will still have ups and downs. Try to anticipate and manage these. Be gentle and accepting of yourself on days when it is just too difficult to see the positive. Treat yourself in the same way as you would a good friend – with the same kindness, care and support.

DEALING WITH BEING BULLIED

Courage is fire, and bullying is smoke. —Benjamin Disraeli

If you're in a relationship or a friendship where you're becoming more and more unhappy and miserable, if you're being bullied or even abused by a colleague, family member or neighbour – in person or through social media – you mustn't use positive thinking as an excuse to stay in a bad situation.

You may be staying in an abusive relationship, for example, because you tell yourself it's the right thing to do for the children; they'll be better off in a family where there are two incomes coming in. Or maybe you've convinced yourself that a bullying colleague can't really help it – they've recently had some personal problems and are clearly very stressed.

That's not positive thinking. It's delusional thinking. Positive thinking does not mean ignoring real difficulties. If someone is persistently badgering, dominating or intimidating you, someone is continually coercing and threatening you, criticising or humiliating you, tyrannising you or making abusive remarks and insulting you, you *must* do something. This person will not go away!

Shift your perspective – use positive thinking to think about the good things that can happen if you do what you know to be the right thing, and that is to get out of the relationship. See leaving a bully or abusive person as a goal. An urgent goal.

In Practice

Bullying is a horrible thing. It sticks with you forever. It poisons you. But only if you let it. —Heather Brewer

Get information, advice and support. Staying silent and telling no one will only isolate you while at the same time empowering the bully or abuser, so you must get help and support. Don't be afraid to tell someone. There are people who can give you support and advice, especially if they've been in a similar situation. There are organisations that specialise in supporting anyone who is being bullied, stalked or abused. Start by going to www.nationalbullyinghelpline.co.uk or phone them on 0845 22 55 787. If you're experiencing domestic abuse, go to www.nationaldomesticviolencehelpline.org.uk or phone 0808 2000 247. If you're being stalked, go to www.stalkinghelpline.org or call the helpline on 0808 802 0300.

Walk away. As well as getting help, support and advice, you need to seriously consider leaving – leaving the job, the relationship or the social media account. Walking away is often the best thing to do, for in doing so, you put yourself in a positive position: one of being in control. You take away the opportunity for the bully or abuser to continue their behaviour. Of course, you might have to walk away from a good job, financial stability, a nice home or a network of social media contacts, but focus on the positive: that you've left the bully or abuser behind. Once you have left them, instead of trying to please, pacify or avoid the bully or abuser, you can put your energy into finding a new job or somewhere to live.

Know that you do have a choice about how to respond. You don't have to put up with a bad, risky or harmful situation. Think about keeping yourself safe and sane and moving forward towards a better life. Identify the good things that can happen if you remove yourself from the misery of the situation. By removing yourself, you put yourself in a positive position: you are in control.

HAVING COURAGE

'Go back?' he thought. 'No good at all! Go sideways? Impossible! Go forward? Only thing to do! On we go!' So up he got, and trotted along with his little sword held in front of him and one hand feeling the wall, and his heart all of a patter and a pitter. —J.R.R. Tolkien, The Hobbit

Having courage doesn't mean not being afraid. Courage means doing something *despite* being afraid. Fear and courage go together. Whenever you're courageous, you're overcoming a fear. To overcome fear, you need courage. Courage is strength in the face of fear. It's strength in spite of uncertainty, in spite of other people's objections or disapproval, hostility or intimidation.

Positive thinking is inherent in courage, it's an inseparable aspect of courage. It's thinking 'I *can* do this' or 'I *will* do this' and 'I *can* cope and I *can* manage'.

Think of a situation in the past when you felt afraid yet faced your fear, took action and things worked out ok. What helped? What was it that made you take that bold step? What did other people do or say that helped give you courage? What did you think or feel?

Now think of a situation you are facing currently that scares you or makes you feel anxious. What are you most afraid of? You might, for example, be afraid of telling someone how you feel, or you might be anxious about asking difficult questions that help you and others face a reality. Perhaps you're afraid of jeopardising your job if you report an injustice, unethical practice or abuse of power or resources. Remind yourself that you have been courageous before and you *can* summon up your courage again.

Whether it's leaving your job or a relationship, standing up for yourself or someone else, giving a speech or performing, speaking out against something, walking into a room full or strangers or making a journey on your own somewhere new, courage is what makes you brave and helps you move forward.

In Practice

You gain strength, courage, and confidence by every experience in which you really stop to look fear in the face. You are able to say to yourself, 'I lived through this horror. I can take the next thing that comes along'.
—Eleanor Roosevelt

Think of how you'll benefit from using your courage – what you'll achieve and how good you'll feel. Focusing on why you're doing something and what you want to achieve – keeping that in your mind – can help prevent feelings of doubt, uncertainty and fear from taking over and can give you the surge of motivation you need to take the necessary first step. Rather than fighting feelings of fear and doubt, acknowledge and accept them. Tell yourself, 'I'm feeling scared. I'm not sure about this'. Then push past those thoughts and feelings and tell yourself, 'But I can do this'.

Plan what you're going to do or say. There's no need to do this in detail, simply think through what you probably need to do – the steps you'll need to take. Visualise yourself successfully doing or saying it.

Don't overthink it. The more you think about whether you should or shouldn't and the longer you have to come up with excuses, the more time you'll have to get yourself scared.

You can't be that kid standing at the top of the waterslide, overthinking it. You have to go down the chute. —Tina Fey

Courage can be prone to leaking, which means the longer you wait, the less of it you'll have. So, once you've decided to do something, don't wait to feel no fear, just act as if you're feeling brave and confident and get on with it.

Focus on the first step. Having thought through the steps, now just focus on that first step, on saying, for example, 'We need to talk' rather than on worrying about how the talk will go. So often, taking the first step is half the battle, so pushing yourself over the threshold will create the momentum that will move things forward – and by then you'll just be dealing with it. It's an exponential process; you only have to start acting with courage – start with a small step – and your courage will increase at a steady rate.

Practise being courageous – choose to do something slightly scary. Write down five things that make you uncomfortable. It might include doing something new or going somewhere you've never been before. Or it might be speaking up and saying what's in your heart. Do one of these at a time – feel the fear and then do it.

COPING WITH CRITICISM

Criticism may not be agreeable, but it is necessary. It fulfils the same function as pain in the human body. It calls attention to an unhealthy state of things. —Winston Churchill

We've all heard of 'constructive' criticism, but if you're like most people, you rarely respond positively to even the most well-meant of criticisms. At best we interpret a criticism as a negative judgement about something we've said or done, and at worst we receive criticism as a personal attack.

Of course, it doesn't feel great to be told you're not doing, looking, saying or behaving as someone else thinks you should. Criticism can cause you stress and upset and trigger the sort of negative thinking that causes resentment and erodes your self-esteem and confidence.

In some cases, the criticism isn't fair and has more to do with the other person's issues and expectations. It's not a criticism, it's verbal abuse – insulting, offensive and damaging. But in other cases, the criticism is justified – it's something you may need to consider and act on.

What's the difference between criticism and verbal abuse? Verbal abuse fails to provide any suggestions as to what it is that you can improve on. As in this example: 'You're hopeless – a waste of bloody time and space – you never get things right. You stupid idiot'. Constructive criticism, however, describes behaviour that can be improved on. For example: 'This is no good. It's *not* what I asked you to do. Please do it the way I showed you and make sure it's done on time'.

Being on the receiving end of criticism isn't easy, but although other people might not be skilled at giving criticism, you *can* learn how to handle it and respond more positively.

In Practice

Let me never fall into the vulgar mistake of dreaming that I am persecuted whenever I am contradicted. —Ralph Waldo Emerson

Clarify the problem and the solution. If you're not clear about what the critic is accusing you of, rephrase what they've said in your own words. 'I just want to be clear, are you saying…?' or 'I'm not sure I've understood, do you think I…?'

Could it be true? Imagine that someone said to you: 'You're *always* late! You *never* turn up on time. You've always got some crap excuse. You don't ever consider anyone else!' Could any of it be true? Often, you can react so quickly to their hostility and exaggerations that you don't stop to consider that there might be some truth in what they're saying. Criticism opens you up to other people's perspectives and interpretations of you – what you think, say and do. Ok, it might not all be accurate, or the other person may be harsh and have exaggerated (critics often do when they're upset, frustrated or angry), but you need to look for seeds of truth in criticism.

If they haven't said so already, ask them what they want you to do about it. Doing this is important because you're making a genuine attempt at finding out how the other person thinks you can put things right and improve the situation. You don't have to agree with their solution, however.

Decide whether or not it's fair and valid and what your response will be. You can see the truth in all or some of the criticism and as a result, change your behaviour. Calmly tell the other person that you understand that's how they see things and explain how or why their criticism is unfair or wrong. Or say nothing and let it go. Most likely their mind is already made up and if you try to argue, you will just be adding fuel to the fire.

Know that there are two ways you can get something positive from criticism. You can see the truth in all or some of the criticism and as a result, change your behaviour. If, though, you think the criticism isn't valid and true, identifying how and why it's invalid can strengthen your beliefs and motivate you to stick to what feels true to you and what, for you, is right and best.

FORGIVING

Forgiveness is giving up the hope that the past could have been any different. —Oprah Winfrey

When somebody wrongs you – either by accident or on purpose – it can be hard to get over it. Whether someone spilt red wine on your sofa or they scraped your car or it's something more serious – a family member or friend betrayed you, a colleague spread some nasty untruths about you, or a partner has been unfaithful – whoever and whatever it was, when you're feeling let down, angry or betrayed, the idea of forgiving someone can feel as if you're giving in and letting them get away with it.

But forgiving someone doesn't mean you're excusing what they said or did; it doesn't mean there's nothing further to work out in the relationship or that everything is ok now.

Forgiveness is first and foremost for *your* benefit – your peace of mind – not for the person who hurt or offended you.

Forgiveness means letting go of the negativity – the resentment, frustration or anger – that you feel as a result of someone else's actions. It involves no longer wanting punishment, revenge, requital or compensation. It means recognising that you've already been hurt once, so you don't need to let the offence, the hurt and the pain keep hurting you by holding on to it.

Not forgiving is like deliberately keeping a wound open – it remains raw and it festers. When you forgive, you allow yourself to heal.

In Practice

To forgive is to set a prisoner free and discover that the prisoner was you. —Lewis B. Smedes

If you're mad, be mad. Don't hide and suppress your feelings. Let it all out. But if you're done with being upset, if you've now reached a point where you are sick of thinking about it and you want to put someone's actions behind you and move on, there are a number of steps you can take:

- **Accept what happened and how it affected you.** No doubt the other person is responsible for their actions and you wish that what they did had never happened. But you can't change what has already taken place. Accept that. If you can recognise and accept that nothing can change what they did, you've taken the first step.
- **Identify any positive aspects.** Maybe other people were helpful and supportive when this person betrayed, hurt or offended you? Maybe, if you've now cut this person from your life, you realise how much better off you are without them.
- **Think about what you learned from the experience.** What would you do differently to avoid becoming involved in a similar situation?
- **Write it down.** You might find it helpful to write an honest, emotional letter telling the other person how hurt and angry you are. Then crumple it up and burn it. As you watch the smoke rise, imagine it carrying your hurt and disappointment into the air – let it go.
- **Change the story you replay to yourself and to other people.** Each time you go back over what happened, you return to negative thoughts and images. Change your story to one that tells of your decision to forgive – to accept and learn from what happened, to identify any positive aspects and move on.
- **Know that your forgiveness could help to mend a relationship.** Forgiving the other person might lead them to acknowledge their wrongdoing and perhaps seek to change their ways *because* they've been forgiven.
- **Be patient.** Know that the process of forgiving – accepting and learning from what happened, identifying any positive aspects and moving on – might happen quite quickly or it may be a gradual process.

CHANGING YOUR MIND

It is well for people who think, to change their minds occasionally in order to keep them clean. —Luther Burbank

Ever changed your mind about something? Of course you have!

Maybe you were enjoying a book, a film or TV series but halfway through, you changed your mind – you decided it wasn't so good after all. So, you simply stopped reading or watching and did something else.

But when it comes to bigger issues – deciding that, actually, you don't want to vote for that party, buy or rent that flat, live in that area, want the job or place at university, or you do want a baby, or you don't want to marry that person – you struggle to change course.

Why is that?

Maybe you're thinking about all the time, effort, love or money you've already put into something. You feel you can't let that go to waste, so you might as well carry on. Perhaps you don't want to admit that you made the wrong decision in the first place. Or it could be that you're worried about letting people down if you pull out of a commitment.

Changing one's mind is often seen as a negative thing – that you're weak, that you're unreliable and can't be depended on.

Not so!

It could be that you realised you jumped ahead of yourself and made a decision too quickly. Or what you thought you wanted to do doesn't now seem such a good idea now – new information has come to light and you realise it's not the right decision after all. Perhaps your circumstances have changed and you have different options. It could be that what you've now changed your mind to do is more in line with your abilities, is more realistic and achievable.

Think positive! Rather than saying you've changed your mind, see it as having made a new decision. As American philosopher and psychologist William James said, 'If you can change your mind, you can change your life'.

In Practice

Make up your mind about things, by all means – but if something happens to show that you are wrong, then it is feeble not to change your mind. Only the strongest people have the pluck to change their minds, and say so.
—Enid Blyton

Free yourself from commitments and situations that are making you unhappy. Instead of thinking you 'ought' to stick with a decision you made a while back, think about what you'd really rather do now. What's more important to you now, more in line with your values and priorities? What's more likely to make you happy? Be honest with yourself.

If you think that your original decision was a mistake, know that at the time, you made the right choice, but now you realise it's not working out for you. You're not a bad person, it's just that your feelings have changed.

Think positive. Tell yourself that changing your mind isn't something worthy of shame or remorse. Instead of regarding yourself as weak and indecisive, see yourself as self-aware, open-minded, flexible and able to change and adapt according to new information and circumstances.

Remind yourself to see your change of mind as you having made a new decision.

Move forward. Once you know you've had a change of heart, acknowledge what you have to lose by letting go but focus on what you have to gain. Start planning how you can act on your new decision. Then take the first step.

Be considerate. If someone else is going to be worse off as a result of you changing your mind, tell them as soon as you can. Don't make lots of excuses. Just be truthful and explain why you've changed your mind. Apologise and say what, if anything, you can do to compensate.

It might not be easy when you've got to explain your change of mind to friends, family or colleagues – but having a few uncomfortable conversations is a small price to pay for what's right for you from now on. The other people will adjust; people can and will sort it out. But if you stay in that situation, you'll feel trapped and unhappy, stuck in a situation you don't like and unable to get on with what you now want to do.

DEALING WITH GUILT

Every man is guilty of all the good he did not do. —Voltaire

Although feelings of guilt or shame can be distressing, like all emotions, guilt has a positive intent – to prompt you to put right something you did or said that has hurt or offended someone else. If, for example, you felt guilty about having pulled out of a friend's special occasion, then your guilt can prompt you to make it up to them in some way.

If you never felt emotions such as guilt, regret, remorse or shame, why would you care about how your actions could affect others? Guilt becomes a negative, harmful emotion only when you allow it to overwhelm you to such an extent that it paralyses you and you fail to do anything to put things right.

Guilt can occur as a result of a wide range of events. Perhaps you lost or broke something belonging to a friend or family member? Maybe you let someone down, said something derogatory or unkind? Perhaps you've been irritated and impatient with your children, or you don't call or visit a family member as often as you think you should.

Whatever it is you did or didn't do, you feel as though you did wrong and now you feel like crap! And the more you replay events in your mind, the worse you seem to make them. It's like a Chinese Whispers game going on in your head – the more you replay it, the more distorted it becomes.

Hanging onto guilt serves no purpose. You have to forgive yourself and do something constructive, something to improve the situation. You can do that by accepting what you did or didn't do, doing something to make amends, learning from what happened and moving on.

In Practice

There's no problem so awful, that you can't add some guilt to it and make it even worse.
—Bill Watterson

Don't be too hard on yourself. There may have been mitigating circumstances, you may have had no option but to do what you did, you may have been unable to get time off work to get to your child's school play, you may have been stressed when you made a critical remark, it may have been a complete accident that you broke something belonging to someone else.

Don't try to shift the blame. Do accept and acknowledge the extent to which you were responsible. Don't try to justify what you did. If what you did wrong affected someone else, accept and acknowledge their pain without minimising it, without excuses and without revisiting all the details of the situation.

Say sorry. Say what, specifically, you're sorry for. Are you sorry for not turning up to their party, or are you sorry that they felt so let down? Or is it both?

Decide what, if anything, you can do to make up for your actions. If you *are* going to do something, make amends as soon as possible. Whatever it is, keep it in proportion to the wrongdoing. Missed your child's school play? Rather than make up for it by buying them a new computer game, suggest going for an ice-cream after school and listen to them tell you all about the play. If you broke something belonging to someone else, get it fixed or replace it as soon as possible. Make it a priority. If you pulled out of an event with a friend – dinner or a weekend away – be the one to arrange a new date to do something together.

Move on. Hanging on to guilt serves no purpose. Hopefully, the other person will recognise your attempt to make amends, but be prepared for the fact that they might not be ready to do that just yet. If you've done what you can, you'll have to accept that the ball is now in their court.

MOVING ON FROM REGRET

Don't let yesterday take up too much of today. —Will Rogers

Regret arises from thinking and feeling that at some point in the past – an hour ago, a week ago or even years ago – you made a 'wrong' decision to do or not do something. And now you see what you did or didn't do in a different light and feel that, in some way, you lost out.

Regrets often focus on what you didn't do – the missed opportunities – and start with the words 'I wish' and 'I should have'. 'I wish I'd travelled more when I was younger'. 'I should have gone to university'. 'I should have been more patient'. 'I wish I'd taken that job'. 'I wish I'd gone to the party last night'.

Regrets can also be about what you did do but now wish you hadn't. 'I wish I hadn't eaten that last piece of chocolate cake'. 'I shouldn't have left that job'. 'I shouldn't have said that'. You replay scenarios in your head – what you should have done and how much better things would've been if only you had or hadn't done this or said that.

When you're regretful, you're evaluating something that did or didn't happen in the past with the knowledge you have in the present. But it's unfair and unreasonable to take what you know now and use it to berate yourself for what you didn't know, realise or understand then.

Don't let regret keep you stuck, feeling defeated and hopeless. Use your regret in a more constructive way. Feelings of regret offer you an opportunity for learning and change. But in order to do that, you have to let go of the 'should've', 'could've' and 'would've'. Maybe you could or couldn't have done something then, but what are you in a position to do now?

In Practice

I did then what I knew how to do. Now that I know better, I do better.
—*Maya Angelou*

Recognise that you can't change what did or didn't happen. Remember, you did what you did or didn't do according to the circumstances and what you knew at the time.

Look for the lessons. What did you learn about yourself? What did you learn about someone else?

Think positively. Turn your thoughts to considering how to do things differently from now on. When you catch yourself having a regretful thought, add a positive thought to it. Here are some examples:

'I should've phoned, so instead I'm going to…'
'I wish I'd ordered something else on the menu but now I'm going to…'
'I should've gone to university but now I'm going to…'
'I wish I'd travelled more when I was younger. But now I'm…'

Remember the power of adding the word 'but' after a negative statement – it leads to a positive sentence.

Ask yourself what can help you to move on. Is there support you need? Is there a conversation you need to have? Are there some boundaries you need to set?

Forgive yourself. Just like the rest of us, you make mistakes. Let go of the idea that you should get it right every time. As the rapper and actor Queen Latifah has said, 'I made decisions that I regret, and I took them as learning experiences… I'm human, not perfect, like anybody else'.

COPING WITH WORRY AND ANXIETY

Worry; to think about problems or unpleasant things that might happen in a way that makes you feel unhappy and frightened. dictionary.cambridge.org

We all know what it's like to feel worried and anxious – to feel fearful at the thought of going for a job interview or taking an exam, for example. Maybe there's been something worrying you recently? Perhaps you've been fretting about the results of a medical test? Maybe you've been getting anxious about giving a presentation, making a journey or attending a social event – a party, a wedding or a school reunion?

Whatever it's about, when you're worried or anxious, doubts, fears and negative possibilities overwhelm your mind. You feel you have no control over what could happen, how events might turn out and whether or not you'll be able to cope if things do go wrong.

Is there a difference between worry and anxiety? Worry is usually about specific things and is relatively short-lived. Anxiety may be more or less intense but longer lasting.

But whether it's worry or anxiety you're feeling, like all emotions, worry and anxiety do have a positive intent – they serve as your internal alarm, to prompt you to do whatever might help to prevent the worst-case scenario from happening.

In Practice

Don't worry about the future; or worry, but know that worrying is as effective as trying to solve an algebra equation by chewing bubblegum. —Mary Schmich

Learn to plan instead of worry. Worry involves your mind going over and over the same problem but doing nothing about it. A good plan, though, can prepare you and provide solutions if things do start going wrong. So, identify what, exactly, it is that you're worried about. What's the worst that can happen? If, for example, you were feeling concerned about making a car journey on your own, you might be worried about getting lost or you might stress that your car could break down.

Look for solutions. Focus on what you *can* do something about rather than on aspects of the situation that are beyond your control. Find one small step you can take *now*. If it was a car journey, you might make sure your phone was fully charged and that you also had a map in case the satnav let you down. You could join a car breakdown service. Once you start doing something about the problem, you may feel less worried because you're putting things in place in case the worst does happen.

Once you have a plan, if you find yourself worrying, tell yourself, 'Stop! I have a plan!' Keep your thoughts on that. Visualise a positive outcome – create images for yourself where you see yourself coping and things turning out well.

Do something positive. Think about what sorts of activities you can turn to in order to switch off from worrying – especially when you need to stop worrying about something you can do nothing about. It could be an activity you can dip into for ten minutes or it could be something you can immerse yourself in for an hour or more. It could be something calming like listening to music, reading a novel, watching a film, doing a puzzle – a crossword or sudoku – or playing a computer game. Maybe you like writing? For some ideas on what to write about, go to www.writersdigest.com/prompts.

Or you could get moving – go for a brisk walk, a run, a bike ride, or have a game of tennis. It could be housework – cleaning the bathroom or kitchen, vacuuming, making beds, cleaning windows or gardening. Whatever it is, for as long as you do it, you make it difficult for worrying thoughts to find their way into your head.

MANAGING ENVY

Envy is the art of counting the other fellow's blessings instead of your own. —Harold Coffin

Envy is that feeling of disappointment, frustration and resentment that we experience when we don't have – but want – something that someone else has. There's always someone we know who has it better than us. Someone who's more skilled, more talented, has more money, more happiness or a family who are more supportive than yours.

Maybe you've felt envious because someone else got the opportunity that you had hoped for – the promotion, the job, the house or the new partner. Perhaps you get envious about something that you know is trivial but still stings – for example, when you read your friends' and colleagues' social media posts and see they get more 'likes' than you do. It's not fair!

Whatever it is that someone else has that you don't, you compare your situation with theirs and find that your situation comes up short.

But comparing yourself with someone else – who they are and what they have – means you can see only what they've got and what you have not. Feelings of inadequacy can turn into resentment and bitterness towards others. Envy can make you lose touch with who you are. Comparing what you don't have with what others do have will only make you miserable – you doubt yourself, your abilities and your achievements.

So, is there anything positive about envy? *Yes.* Instead of letting it keep you stuck thinking about what you don't have, envy can motivate and inspire you to improve your situation and to achieve your goals.

In Practice

Three be the things I shall never attain: envy, content, and sufficient champagne. —Dorothy Parker

Recognise envy. The next time you find yourself resenting what someone else has, recognise it for what it is: envy.

Accept it. If it's not possible to have what the other person has – naturally curly hair, the ability to sing like an angel or to write a best-selling novel – accept it and turn your attention to what you *do* have and what you *can* achieve.

Use your envy to create a goal. Rather than wallow in thoughts such as 'Why have they got it? It's not fair', change your focus. Start planning how you can work towards what it is they've got that you want. Even if you can't attain exactly what the other person has – a supportive family, for example – you can find other ways to achieve it – develop supportive friendships, for instance. This will help you be more positive since you are no longer comparing what the other person has with what you haven't. Instead, you'll be working towards what you want and what, in your circumstances, is more realistic for you to achieve.

Get some perspective. When it comes to people's social media posts, you rarely read about someone's arguments with their partner, the job they hate or their children's bad exam results. Most people show you what they want you to see – an edited, glossy version of their life. So, the next time you feel envious about someone else's life, remember that you're looking at only part of the story. Instead of thinking, 'It's all right for them, they've got such a happy life', see the whole picture and recognise that the other person may not have everything they want and that they have their problems too.

MAKING NEW FRIENDS

A friend may be waiting behind a stranger's face. —Maya Angelou

Do you know someone who makes new friends wherever they go? Their breezy self-confidence attracts people to them like a magnet. For many of us, though, making friends isn't so easy.

Maybe you've moved to a new area, you're working in a new job or you've become a new parent and you'd like to befriend some like-minded people. Perhaps you want to hook up with others to share common interests or you want new friends for fun or support.

Perhaps you're lonely and you simply want to connect with people, to be accepted, included and involved. Maybe you're looking for companionship and support. Or you just want to go to the cinema and be sitting next to someone you know.

Numerous studies show that one of the most positive things we can do for our well-being is to connect with other people. Friendships are important for our well-being. Humans are inherently social creatures, we're wired to benefit from close relationships – to make attachments – with other people.

Most of us make use of some form of social media, giving us a constant opportunity to share details of our lives with dozens, if not hundreds, of 'friends'. But friends that are solely virtual aren't the same as friendships in the real world.

It takes effort on your part – you need to be willing to meet others, to be yourself and give something of yourself. You *can* make new friends, but you can't wait for other people to come to you. You need to get out there!

In Practice

You can't stay in your corner of the Forest waiting for others to come to you. You have to go to them sometimes. —A.A. Milne, Winnie-the-Pooh

Start with your interests. When you have interests and activities you enjoy, you can meet people with similar interests. Whether it's tennis or train spotting, it makes it easier for you to talk to others and make friends *because* you share similar interests and values. Find others like you. Discover where the other knitters, singers, hikers or bookworms are. Go to www.meetup.com, which will enable you to find and join groups of people in your local area who share your interests. There are groups to fit a wide range of interests and hobbies, plus others you'll never have thought of. There are book groups, art groups, film groups and sci-fi groups. Gardening groups, singing groups and cycling groups. People who go to 'meetups' do so knowing they'll be meeting others who are also open to making new friends. If you find people who are just as keen on, for example, board games, photography, football, walking or netball as you are, then you'll find it relatively easy to connect and make friends with them.

Meet your friends' friends. One of the easiest ways to make new friends and expand your social circle is to meet your friends' friends. So ask a friend to invite one or two of their friends to join you the next time you do something together.

Reach out. As you meet and make new friends, take the initiative and at some point invite a couple of people out or over to your house for curry or pizza, to the pub or to an event related to your shared interests.

Volunteer. Volunteering is also a good way to meet people and make friends. By working together, you meet and create bonds with people who want to make a contribution to the lives of others, so you have a common cause. Go to do-it.com for volunteering opportunities in your area.

TAKING RISKS

The problem is the negativity bias; we tend to exaggerate the riskiness of certain moves and underestimate the opportunities of others. —Tim Ferriss

Changing your job or going freelance, downhill mountain biking, cave diving or white-water rafting all involve a risk. So does investing in the stock market, having major heart surgery or going on a blind date. Letting out your home through Airbnb is a risk, as might be travelling in another country on your own or simply going to a café alone.

One way or another, they all expose you to the chance of something going wrong.

Although you might be attracted to a new opportunity – participating in an extreme sport, taking on new responsibilities at work, for example – you worry whether it will be worth the risk, whether things will actually turn out well. You know there's a chance that things will go wrong; there are potential hazards and you could lose out in some way. You're not sure you'll be able to handle the responsibility, stress or consequences that come with taking a risk.

But you take a risk every time you start reading a book you've not read before or a book by an author that's new to you. You take a risk when you decide to watch a new film or try a new restaurant or some dish you've not eaten before. The risk is that the book, the film, the restaurant and the food might not turn out to be as good as you hoped.

Taking a risk can open you up to new ideas, opportunities and experiences. You can discover good things about yourself, your abilities, other people and the world. And, as the writer T.S Eliot, said, *Only those who will risk going too far can possibly find out how far it is possible to go.*

When you take a risk, you make things happen rather than wait for them to happen to you. And the fact that you are taking a risk makes it likely that you will do your damnedest to make sure things *will* work out!

In Practice

Security is mostly a superstition. Life is either a daring adventure or nothing. —Helen Keller

Reduce the risk. Although negative thinking – thinking about the worst that could happen – can prevent you from taking a risk, it can also help you get prepared, to do what you can to minimise that risk. If, for example, you were going to buy a property, you'd hire a surveyor to identify any structural problems so that you could make an informed decision on whether or not to go ahead and buy the place. If you were going to cook a new recipe for a special occasion, you might try out the recipe the week before. So do the same with anything else that involves taking a risk. Of course things could go wrong, so identify the worst-case scenario and then plan how you'd deal with that. Get advice or information, put in the practice, make the safety checks, save the money, have a time limit – whatever you think is relevant and necessary.

Have a plan B. Having a plan B – a contingency plan – helps you be more bold – it enables you to make positive risk-taking decisions. Why? Because you know that you have something to fall back on if it doesn't work out.

Get used to risk – take small risks. Think of three things you could do that would move you out of your comfort zone, things that won't involve too much of a stretch. You could try a new food where the risk is you won't like it. Or you could try a different route to visit family or friends, where the risk is you'll get lost. Or smile at a stranger, where the risk is you'll be ignored.

Trust yourself, make snap decisions. Now and again, don't overthink it, just allow yourself to do something on impulse. Snap decisions instil a feeling of self-trust. Be spontaneous. If you suddenly feel inclined to do something that's a small risk, just do it.

HAVING A POSITIVE BODY IMAGE

I'm not going to sacrifice my mental health to have the perfect body.
—Demi Lovato

Your body image is how you see and what you think about your body and aspects of your body – your shape, height, weight, facial features and so on.

How do you feel about your body? Do you have a positive body image? Your body image affects how you behave, what you do or don't do with your body.

How we each feel about our body and how we think it 'should' look is influenced by what we and others – friends, family, the media, etc. – think is the 'right' body shape and size.

Unfortunately, we're bombarded every day with images of perfection: perfect lives, perfect homes, perfect food and perfect bodies. It can be hard not to compare yourself unfavourably with the body shapes that surround you. But so often, those comparisons and how we see ourselves is unrealistic.

How can you feel positive about your body? Certainly not by starving yourself, sweating and pummelling your body until every inch of it is toned, tanned, firm, fat-free and in the shape you think it 'should' be. It isn't so much down to what your body looks like but how you feel about it that counts. So, if your body image is more negative than positive, you need to reframe the way you view, think and talk about your body.

In Practice

Stop spending all day obsessing, cursing, perfecting your body like it's all you've got to offer the world. —Glennon Doyle Melton

Avoid getting into 'I hate my nose/thighs/teeth/stomach/bum' conversations. Getting caught up in a conversation about the way someone else looks, whether they've put on weight, that they think their arms are flabby, their nose is too big, their face is too lined and so on, inevitably affects the way you view your own body. Before you know it, you're falling into competitive self-criticism – as soon as your friend mentions a flaw, you trump it with one of yours. The next time a friend brings up their body hang-up, change the conversation to focus on your positives. Each come up with three body positives, for yourself and for each other. That way you can both feel better.

Be critically aware of social and media messages, images and attitudes that make you feel bad about your body. Avoid tabloid and gossip media that constantly shame celebrities' bodies. 'The eyes of others our prisons; their thoughts our cages', Virginia Woolf once wrote. She was right. You need to break out and escape with your self-esteem intact. Remind yourself that the perfect media images are unrealistic and unattainable for most of us (and even for the subject of the image, thanks to Photoshop!).

Shift your focus from what your body looks like to what it can do. When you think about yourself in terms of what your body can do, you start to view your body in a very different way. A positive way. Appreciate all that your body can do. Every day your body is working for you: walking, running, lifting and holding, writing and talking, cutting, chopping and stirring. Be thankful for this.

Increase your body's potential – whatever that might be for you. Whatever your body's ability, you can challenge it to a new activity or a new skill. It could be a creative skill – drawing, painting or crafts. It could be physical exercise – yoga, dancing, hiking, cycling or climbing. Exercise ensures that you experience your body from the 'inside' rather than the 'outside' and helps you to appreciate its myriad abilities.

Write down three positive things. Make these things you like about yourself that aren't related to your appearance and remind yourself that your appearance is not 100% of who you are.

AVOIDING THE BLAME GAME

Focus on fixing the problem, never focus on the blame. Problems are only resolved when solutions are sought. —Catherine Pulsifer

Your job, your colleague, your partner or your dysfunctional family. The kids, your dog, your neighbour, the media, the weather or the government. How often have you looked for someone or something to blame for a situation you find yourself in? How often is someone else responsible for a problem you're having?

Something goes wrong or doesn't go the way you expected and you feel disappointed, frustrated, resentful or angry. You feel let down. You see yourself as good and the other person as bad. They're wrong and you're right. It's not fair.

Of course, in many cases it really is someone else's fault. But blaming someone or something else for what goes wrong is, on the one hand, judgemental and vindictive, and on the other hand is casting yourself in the role of the victim, helpless and disempowered. Either way, blaming and finding fault leads to a dead end – it stops you from resolving a situation.

Blaming and berating the other person for getting you both lost in a foreign city, for example, gets you nowhere. Literally! Spending your time working out how you're going to find your way to where you want to go is a far more productive and positive way to deal with the situation.

When you believe that someone else is responsible for the problem, it's easy to think that they're also responsible for putting things right. But if you can see past their wrongdoing, then you can look to yourself for the solution.

In Practice

People are always blaming their circumstances for what they are... (But) The people who get on in this world are the people who get up and look for the circumstances they want, and, if they can't find them, make them. —George Bernard Shaw

Recognise when you're blaming. Whether it's your lack of sleep, a failed internet connection or the wrong directions our friend gave us, too often we can get into a habit of blaming without realising we're doing it. Try to be more aware of the times you say things like 'It's not my fault', 'It's your fault', 'You made me feel...', 'I couldn't, because they...', 'You should have...', 'It's not fair', 'Why did you make me...?' Things go wrong. What you do next is what makes all the difference. Do you look to see who messed up? Do you look for what went wrong? Why? Are you trying to work out what went wrong and how to keep it from going wrong again or are you simply looking for someone or something to blame?

Know that the blame game wastes time. Any time you're busy fixing blame, you're wasting time and energy, not fixing the problem. Once you realise you've been trapped in negative, blaming thoughts – what went wrong or what should have happened – you're free to step out of that trap and more able to find a positive solution.

Take responsibility. Consider the possibility that you somehow contributed to the situation. This doesn't mean nothing or no one else played a part, it just means perhaps you did, as well. You blame your partner because you're out of milk and they always forget to buy milk. So if you know they always forget, why rely on them to buy it? Think of a way to remind them or buy it yourself.

Maybe it was and maybe it wasn't someone else's fault. It doesn't matter. What matters now is what you've learnt, what you do next and what you'd do if a similar situation presented itself again.

Don't sweat the small stuff. So your friend got you both lost, or the hotel room your partner booked isn't what you expected. Is it really that important? Let it go.

BEING NON-JUDGEMENTAL

Those who judge will never understand. And those who understand will never judge. —Author unknown

Do you judge other people, their words and behaviour? Of course you do. It would be impossible not to. You're human. It's what we all do – we judge, assess, form opinions and come to conclusions about others. But when we're being judgemental, more often than not, rather than looking at the pros and cons, we're looking only at the negative aspects of a person or situation.

Too often, we listen to what someone says – their opinions, political or religious beliefs – we see something someone does – the food they eat, the amount they drink, the tattoos they have, the clothes they're wearing, the type of music they listen to, how they bring up their children, the cosmetic surgery they've had – that we don't approve of, understand or agree with and we become critical and judgemental.

We all have ideas about what others 'should' and 'shouldn't' be doing and the way they are 'supposed' to do things. If they're not doing or saying things the way we think they should, we judge their choices as stupid, mad or 'wrong' in some way. And that's the end of it. We don't try to find out more. We don't try to understand. We don't think that they are simply managing a situation in a different way than we would.

It's easy to make assumptions about others that prevent us from respecting them, their situations and their choices. We assume we know the whole story. What, though, if we were able to view other people's circumstances and choices more positively, with an open mind? And not just their circumstances and choices but their failings and foibles, weaknesses and weirdness, too?

In Practice

It's not what you look at that matters. It's what you see.
—Henry David Thoreau

Be aware when you're being judgemental. If what someone says or does leaves you feeling irritated, impatient, disappointed or even angry with them, then you're probably being judgemental. If you think they've brought it on themselves or that they should change their ways, then you're judging them. If you're dismissive about a person's plight, then you're being judgemental. If you talk disparagingly about them, then you're being judgemental.

Instead of judging someone for what they've done or failed to do, try instead to understand the person. For example, the person sleeping rough? What do you really know about how and why a person might be a rough sleeper? And that screaming toddler? Maybe she's screaming because she's unwell or has a learning difficulty, not because she has awful parents who can't control their child.

Empathise. Ask yourself:

* Do I really understand their situation or do I just think I know?
* Can I learn more about their situation?
* If I was being kind, what might I think has caused or motivated them to do or behave like that? What could be a reasonable explanation?

Give them the benefit of the doubt. There may be mitigating circumstances, circumstances which, if you knew about them, would modify your judgement. Try to imagine what might have led to the person's situation and construct the most favourable interpretation that the facts allow. Concede that a person may be justified in behaving the way they do.

Practise responding with kindness and empathy. Next time you read or listen to someone's opinion – on the radio, on TV or in public – and it annoys you, think about giving them the benefit of the doubt. What could be a reasonable explanation for why they've done or said what they did? Believe something good about someone rather than something bad.

COPING WITH CHANGE

Change is the only constant in life. —Heraclitus

The same ancient Greek philosopher who said 'Change is the only constant in life' also illustrated the point about change being ever present when he said, 'No man ever steps in the same river twice, for it's not the same river and he's not the same man'.

It's not just rivers that are constantly changing though. The weather changes, the menu changes. So, does the time the post is delivered, the programme being televised and which political party is in power. But that doesn't mean we welcome or get used to it. In fact, the thought of more serious changes – a major staff reshuffle or changes in procedures at work, redundancy, moving home, good friends or close family moving away – can leave you feeling threatened and vulnerable.

The prospect of change can mean you're facing an uncertain future, not knowing what to expect and often assuming the worst. You worry whether you'll be able to adapt and cope with the change in circumstances. You worry whether things will work out well. Of course, change can be stressful, but so is trying to hold on. Holding on is like swimming against the current – it saps your energy. Energy that could be better spent on moving on.

In Practice

If nothing ever changed, there'd be no butterflies. —Author unknown

Get informed. If you're facing a change, find out what you can about what will be involved. Ask questions and get information about the changes. Get support – talk to friends, family members and colleagues and ask for their ideas. Get the resources you might need, too.

Write a list of all the negative things that you think a change will bring. It's important to acknowledge the negative aspects – don't ignore or deny the challenges and difficulties that the change could bring.

Have positive beliefs and expectations. Now write down the positive things, such as new opportunities, that change brings. Acknowledge and do what you can to prepare for the negative aspects of a change. Then choose to focus on the positive aspects.

Draw on your strengths. Prepare to manage change by drawing on your strengths. What skills, abilities and knowledge do you have that you can use to manage the challenges that the change will bring?

Practise making changes and see that you can adapt. Choosing to break a routine way of doing things on a regular basis can be an effective tactic for coping with the inevitable changes that will occur in your life. Drive, walk or cycle a different route to normal. You could even take a different route around the supermarket for a change. Move the clock or the wastepaper bin to a different place in the room. See how long it takes you to stop looking in the wrong place for the time or to stop throwing rubbish on the floor. What could you do? Start today. Train yourself to manage change.

Identify and hold on to what's unchanging. When you're going through a lot of change, it helps to write down your routine. Having some things in your life that stay the same – walking the dog every day, going for a run at weekends – gives you an 'anchor', a reminder that some things are still the same.

ANSWERS TO IN PRACTICE QUESTIONS IN PART ONE

Understanding the positive intentions of negative thoughts

- The positive intention of anger: anger – a powerful motivating force – can motivate you to put right a wrong, to get what you want. It can also let others know how strongly you feel about something.
- The positive intention of jealousy is to protect you from losing out – to alert you to the fact that you may need to up your game, to make an effort to improve, or to guard against something or someone slipping away from you.
- The positive intention of embarrassment: embarrassment is a sign that you care about how others see you – that you regret what you said or did and that you acknowledge it and are sorry. In other circumstances, embarrassment is a sign that you don't approve and want to distance yourself from what someone else did or said.
- The positive aspect of boredom is to prompt you either to find a new way to engage with and be interested in the situation that is boring you, or, if you can, to leave the situation and do something else.

Recognising cognitive distortions

- No wonder I've made some mistakes with writing this report. What does my manager expect if she won't give me enough time to complete it properly? **Blaming**
- I bet they only asked me to join them because the other person couldn't make it. They obviously didn't want to ask me first. **Mind reading. Jumping to a conclusion**

- I've never used the tube trains in London before. I'll get confused and stressed. I just know I'll get completely lost. I won't know what to do. **Catastrophising. Polarised thinking**
- The person who interviewed me was very nice but all I can think about was the one question I didn't know how to answer. **Tunnel thinking**
- My manager has changed her mind and doesn't need the report after all. So that's another example of how incompetent she is. **Confirmation bias**
- My friend hasn't replied to my texts. I must have done something to upset him. **Jumping to a conclusion**
- If this isn't perfect it will have been a complete waste of time. **Polarised thinking**

MORE POSITIVE
THINKING QUOTES

The pessimist sees difficulty in every opportunity. The optimist sees opportunity in every difficulty. —Winston Churchill

*Things work out best for those who make the best of how things work out.
—John Wooden*

Positive thinking will let you do everything better than negative thinking will. —Zig Ziglar

The primary cause of unhappiness is never the situation, but your thoughts about it. Be aware of the thoughts you are thinking. —Eckhart Tolle

We cannot solve our problems with the same thinking we used when we created them. —Albert Einstein

The world as we have created it, is a process of our thinking. It cannot be changed without changing our thinking. —Albert Einstein

Think for yourself and let others enjoy the privilege of doing so too. —Voltaire

It is the mark of an educated mind to be able to entertain a thought without accepting it. —Aristotle

If you have built castles in the air, your work need not be lost; that is where they should be. Now put the foundations under them. —Henry David Thoreau

The most common way people give up their power is by thinking they don't have any. —Alice Walker

The only limit to the height of your achievements is the reach of your dreams and your willingness to work for them. —Michelle Obama

I am always doing that which I cannot do, in order that I may learn how to do it. —Pablo Picasso

Progress is impossible without change, and those who cannot change their minds cannot change anything. —George Bernard Shaw

Whatever you can do, or dream you can, begin it. Boldness has genius, power and magic in it. —Goethe

Twenty years from now you will be more disappointed by the things you didn't do than by the ones you did. So throw off the bowlines, sail away from the safe harbour, catch the trade winds in your sails. Explore. Dream. Discover.
—Mark Twain

Leap and the net will appear. —Zen saying

Nothing will ever be attempted, if all possible objections must be first overcome. —Samuel Johnson

You measure the size of the accomplishment by the obstacles you have to overcome to reach your goals. —Booker T. Washington

You don't learn to walk by following the rules. You learn by doing, and falling over. —Richard Branson

I have not failed. I've just found 10,000 ways that won't work. —Thomas Edison

Pearls don't lie on the seashore. If you want one, you must dive for it.
—Chinese proverb

Opportunity dances with those on the dance floor. —Author unknown

Do one thing every day that scares you. —Eleanor Roosevelt

Trust your own instinct. Your mistakes might as well be your own, instead of someone else's. —Billy Wilder

If you risk nothing, then you risk everything. —Geena Davis

Take risks: if you win, you will be happy; if you lose, you will be wise.
—Author unknown

The future rewards those who press on. I don't have time to feel sorry for myself. I don't have time to complain. I'm going to press on. —Barack Obama

Don't cry because it's over. Smile because it happened. —Dr Seuss

ABOUT THE AUTHOR

Gill Hasson is a teacher, trainer and writer. She has 20 years' experience in the area of personal development. Her expertise is in the areas of confidence and self-esteem, communication skills, assertiveness and resilience.

Gill delivers teaching and training for educational organisations, voluntary and business organisations, and the public sector.

Gill is the author of the bestselling *Mindfulness* and *Emotional Intelligence*, plus other books on the subjects of dealing with difficult people, resilience, communication skills and assertiveness.

Gill's particular interest and motivation is in helping people to realise their potential, to live their best life! You can contact Gill via her website www.gillhasson.co .uk or email her at gillhasson@btinternet.com.